太阳的远近

# HOW FAR AWAY IS THE SUN?

**and other essays**

READINGS IN
CHINESE
CULTURE SERIES

VOLUME

# 2

INTERMEDIATE MID

第二册

## Weijia Huang 黄伟嘉          Qun Ao 敖群
**Boston University**          **United States Military Academy,
West Point**

CHENG & TSUI COMPANY
Boston

18 17 16 15 14 13 12     2 3 4 5 6 7 8 9 10

Published by
Cheng & Tsui Company, Inc.
25 West Street
Boston, MA 02111-1213 USA
Fax (617) 426-3669
www.cheng-tsui.com
"Bringing Asia to the World"™

ISBN 978-0-88727-535-7

Library of Congress Cataloging-in-Publication Data

Huang, Weijia, 1955-
    How far away is the Sun? / by Weijia Huang and Qun Ao = [Tai yang de yuan jin /
    Huang Weijia, Ao Qun bian xie]
        p. cm. – (Cheng & Tsui readings in Chinese culture ; vol. 2 = Zhong guo yu yan wen hua xi lie ; v 2)
    Includes index.
    ISBN-13: 978-0-88727-535-7
    ISBN-10: 0-88727-535-4 (pbk.)
    1. Chinese language—Textbooks for foreign speakers—English. I. Ao, Qun, 1955- II. Title. III. Title: Tai yang de yuan jin.

PL1129.E5H82 2007
495.1—dc22

                                                                2007060886

# Publisher's Note

The Cheng & Tsui Chinese language Series is designed to publish and widely distribute quality language learning materials created by leading instructors from around the world. We welcome readers' comments and suggestions concerning the publications in this series. Please contact the following members of our Editorial Board, in care of our Editorial Department (e-mail: **editor@cheng-tsui.com**).

Professor Shou-hsin Teng, Chief Editor
Graduate Institute of Teaching Chinese as a Second Language
National Taiwan Normal University

Professor Dana Scott Bourgerie
Department of Asian and Near Eastern Languages
Brigham Young University

Professor Samuel Cheung
Department of Chinese
Chinese University of Hong Kong

Professor Ying-che Li
Department of East Asian Languages and Literatures
University of Hawaii

Professor Timothy Light
Department of Comparative Religion
Western Michigan University

# Cheng & Tsui Titles of Related Interest

**The Way of Chinese Characters**
The Origins of 400 Essential Words
*By Jianhsin Wu; Illustrated by Chen Zheng and Chen Tian*
ISBN: 978-0-88727-527-2

**Pop Chinese**
A Cheng & Tsui Bilingual Handbook of Contemporary Colloquial Expressions
*By Yu Feng, Yaohua Shi, Zhijie Jia, Judith M. Amory, and Jie Cai*
ISBN: 978-0-88727-563-0

**Tales & Traditions**
Readings in Chinese Literature Series Volume 1
*Adapted by Yun Xiao, Hui Xiao, and Ying Wang*
ISBN: 978-0-88727-534-0

**Chinese BuilderCards**
The Lightning Path to Mastering Vocabulary
*By Song Jiang and Haidan Wang*
Simplified Characters          ISBN: 978-0-88727-434-3
Traditional Characters         ISBN: 978-0-88727-426-8

**Cheng & Tsui Chinese Character Dictionary**
A Guide to the 2000 Most Frequently Used Characters
*Huidi Wang, Editor-in-Chief*
ISBN: 978-0-88727-314-8

*See www.cheng-tsui.com for more information about these and other titles of interest to Chinese language learners.*

# ◆ 目录 ◆
## ◆ 目錄 ◆

Contents

# Preface

Despite the variety of Chinese textbooks available today, the need for a coherent sequence of reading materials, suitable for multiple levels of Chinese proficiency, remains. Cheng & Tsui Company recently invited us to develop such a series, starting from beginning Chinese and proceeding to advanced—a challenge we were delighted to meet.

This series of reading materials shall consist of five volumes, corresponding to five progressive levels of Chinese proficiency. Volume one is suitable for use by students in the second semester of their first year of Chinese study, or at the "Intermediate Low" level, according to ACTFL proficiency guidelines (please visit **www.actfl.org** for more information). Volumes two and three are designed for students in the first and second semesters, respectively, of their second year of study, or levels "Intermediate Mid" and "Intermediate High." Volumes four and five are appropriate for students in the first and second semesters, respectively, of third year Chinese: "Advanced Low" and "Advanced Mid."

*How Far Away Is the Sun?* is the second volume of this Cheng & Tsui Chinese Essay Series. It is intended for students in the first semester of a second year Chinese course.

Each volume consists of ten lessons. The text of each lesson is approximately five hundred characters in length and has a list of approximately thirty new vocabulary items. The vocabulary lists were chosen based on popular, standard Chinese language textbooks, and selections were further solidified after field-testing. Exercises are provided at the end of each lesson in a variety of formats: matching related words, multiple-choice, questions covering essay content, and discussion questions for oral practice. Answer keys and a vocabulary index can be found at the end of each volume.

To accommodate a diverse range of proficiency levels and learning practices, each lesson also includes a list of frequently used words that are similar in meaning to vocabulary items, or otherwise related to the essay. In an appendix at the back of this book, the full text of each essay is also provided in pinyin, together with simplified Chinese characters, in consideration of various language levels and teaching styles. Furthermore, each lesson's text, vocabulary, and exercises are printed on facing pages in both simplified and traditional characters. The answers keys and index also provide both character forms.

We wrote the essays such that the prose not only conforms to standard Mandarin Chinese, but also retains a smooth and straightforward flow. To ensure that students continue to review previously learned material, later lessons incorporate grammar patterns and vocabulary words that appear in earlier lessons.

At present, many American high schools have begun to offer an Advanced Placement (AP) Program in Chinese, and the AP curriculum specifically emphasizes the need for students to understand and appreciate Chinese culture while studying the language. In preparing this series of reading materials, we made a concerted effort to ensure that linguistic practice is seamlessly integrated with the acquisition of cultural knowledge, so that students may understand both contemporary and historical Chinese culture through language learning. In order to accurately reflect both

China's historic traditions and modern trends, all essays that refer to classical stories include the original text along with its source. We also consulted various relevant materials and verified facts for all lessons that discuss present-day social issues.

We believe that students will find these compiled essays both intellectually stimulating and engaging. Our goal is that this series' lessons will help students broaden their linguistic range, stimulate their interest in learning Chinese, boost their reading comprehension level, and strengthen their understanding of Chinese culture.

We sincerely hope this series of reading materials will be of use to all students of Chinese—whether they are taking AP Chinese language and culture courses in high school, are enrolled in Chinese language courses in college, or are studying Chinese independently.

We want to thank Cheng & Tsui Company for giving us the opportunity to create this series and for making many valuable suggestions. Our sincere thanks also go to Melina Packer and Kristen Wanner, of the Cheng & Tsui editorial department, for their great support and excellent work on this project. We are very grateful to Dr. Matthew Fraleigh, a professor at Brandeis University, for proofreading the English preface. Our gratitude also extends to Mr. Jian Liu for his excellent illustrations in this volume. We also want to thank Xi Huang and Bei Kang for their contributions to this project.

Any comments or criticisms from teachers and students alike would be gladly welcomed. These insights would be invaluable for the improvement of future editions of this book. Please direct any comments to: **editor@cheng-tsui.com**.

Weijia Huang and Qun Ao
June 2007
Boston

# 编写说明

　　现在用于课堂语法教学的中文教材很多，但是缺少合适的不同层次的阅读教材，波士顿剑桥出版社约我们编写一套从初级到高级的阅读教材，我们便欣然应承了下来。

　　这套教材共五册，涵盖五个不同的阶段。第一册适用于一年级第二学期，按照美国外语教学委员会(ACTFL)的语言标准，大致属于中低级水平；第二册适用于二年级第一学期，属于中中级水平；第三册适用于二年级第二学期，属于中高级水平；第四册适用于三年级第一学期，属于高低级水平；第五册适用于三年级第二学期，属于高中级水平。本册《太阳的远近》是第二册。

　　每一册有十篇课文，每篇课文500字左右，有30个生词。词汇的选用参考了常用的同等水平的汉语课本。每课后面有练习，练习包括词语连接，选择答案，思考讨论等形式。每册后面有练习答案和生词索引。

　　为了帮助学生阅读，书后面附有拼音课文；为了扩展学生的词汇量，生词后面列有与课文内容相关的常用同类词语；为了照顾使用不同字体的学生，课文、生词、练习以及答案都采用繁简两种形式。

# 編寫說明

　　現在用於課堂語法教學的中文教材很多，但是缺少合適的不同層次的閱讀教材，波士頓劍橋出版社約我們編寫一套從初級到高級的閱讀教材，我們便欣然應承了下來。

　　這套教材共五冊，涵蓋五個不同的階段。第一冊適用於一年級第二學期，按照美国外語教学委員会(ACTFL)的語言標准，大致屬于中低級水平；第二冊适用於二年級第一學期，屬于中中級水平；第三冊适用於二年級第二學期，屬于中高級水平；第四冊适用於三年級第一學期，屬于高低級水平；第五冊适用於三年級第二學期，屬于高中級水平。本冊《太陽的遠近》是第二冊。

　　每一冊有十篇課文，每篇課文500字左右，有30個生詞。詞彙的選用參考了常用的同等水平的汉语課本。每課後面有練習，練習包括詞語連接，選擇答案，思考討論等形式。每冊後面有練習答案和生詞索引。

　　為了幫助學生閱讀，書後面附有拼音課文；為了擴展學生的詞匯量，生詞後面列有與課文內容相關的常用同類詞語；為了照顧使用不同字體的學生，課文、生詞、練習以及答案都採用繁簡兩種形式。

在课文撰写中，我们力求做到遣词造句合乎语法规范，行文平实通顺流畅。为了让学生能够反复练习语法和词语，后面课文尽量重复前面课文的语法点和生词。

现在美国的中学即将开始中文AP课程，中文AP课程强调学生在学习中文的同时了解中国文化，我们在编写这套教材时就特别注重语言实践和文化体认相结合。

为了准确地表现中国传统文化和现代文化，课文中凡是涉及到古文的都附有原文和出处；凡是阐述现代社会问题的观点都查阅了文献；相关的信息诸如年代、数字等也都作了核实。

本教材编写宗旨是：通过一系列知识性和趣味性的课文，开阔学生学习中文的空间；激发学生学习中文的兴趣；提高学生阅读中文的水平；增强学生理解中国文化的能力。我们希望这套系列阅读教材，对于参加中文AP课程的中学生和选修中文课的大学生以及自学中文的人都能有所帮助。

我们感谢波士顿剑桥出版社给我们这次机会来编写这套教材，感谢Melina Packer小姐和Kristen Wanner女士为本书编辑做了大量的工作。我们也感谢布兰黛斯大学马修凡教授帮助我们修改前言的英文部分，感谢刘健先生为本书绘制了精美的插图，我们还感谢黄兮和康贝为本书作出的贡献。因为我们水平有限，错误之处还请老师和同学指正。

黄伟嘉 敖群 2007年6月于波士顿

在課文撰寫中，我們力求做到遣詞造句合乎語法規範，行文平實通順流暢。為了讓學生能夠反複練習語法和詞語，後面課文盡量重複前面課文的語法點和生詞。

　　現在美國的中學即將開始中文AP課程，中文AP課程強調學生在學習中文的同時了解中國文化，我們在編寫這套教材時就特別注重語言實踐和文化体認相結合。

　　為了準確地表現中國傳統文化和現代文化，課文中凡是涉及到古文的都附有原文和出處；凡是闡述現代社會問題的觀點都查閱了文獻；相關的信息諸如年代、數字等也都作了核實。

　　本教材編寫宗旨是：通過一系列知識性和趣味性的課文，開闊學生學習中文的空間；激發學生學習中文的興趣；提高學生閱讀中文的水平；增強學生理解中國文化的能力。我們希望這套系列閱讀教材，對於參加中文AP課程的中學生和選修中文課的大學生以及自學中文的人都能有所幫助。

　　我們感謝波士頓劍橋出版社給我們這次机會來編寫這套教材，感謝Melina Packer小姐和Kristen Wanner女士為本書編輯做了大量的工作。我們也感謝布蘭黛斯大學馬修凡教授幫助我們修改前言的英文部分，感謝劉健先生為本書繪制了精美的插圖，我們還感謝黃分和康貝為本書作出的貢獻。因為我們水平有限，錯誤之處還請老師和同學指正。

黃偉嘉　敖群　2007年6月於波士頓

# ◆ 词类简称表 ◆
## ◆ 詞類簡稱表 ◆

## Abbreviations of Parts of Speech

| Part of Speech | English Definition | Simplified Characters | Traditional Characters | Pinyin |
|---|---|---|---|---|
| *n.* | noun | 名词 | 名詞 | míngcí |
| *v.* | verb | 动词 | 動詞 | dòngcí |
| *aux.* | auxiliary verb | 助动词 | 助動詞 | zhùdòngcí |
| *vo.* | verb-object | 动宾词组 | 動賓詞組 | dòngbīncízǔ |
| *vc.* | verb complement structure | 动补结构 | 動補結構 | dòngbǔjiégòu |
| *adj.* | adjective | 形容词 | 形容詞 | xíngróngcí |
| *pn.* | pronoun | 代词 | 代詞 | dàicí |
| *m.* | measure word | 量词 | 量詞 | liàngcí |
| *num.* | numeral | 数词 | 數詞 | shùcí |
| *adv.* | adverb | 副词 | 副詞 | fùcí |
| *prep.* | preposition | 介词 | 介詞 | jiècí |
| *prep...o.* | preposition-object | 介词结构 | 介詞結構 | jiècíjiégòu |
| *conj.* | conjunction | 连词 | 連詞 | liáncí |

| Part of Speech | English Definition | Simplified Characters | Traditional Characters | Pinyin |
|---|---|---|---|---|
| *par.* | particle | 助词 | 助詞 | zhùcí |
| *int.* | interjection | 叹词 | 嘆詞 | tàncí |
| *id.* | idioms | 成语 | 成語 | chéngyǔ |
| *prn.* | proper noun | 专用名词 | 專用名詞 | zhuànyòngmíngcí |
| *ce.* | common expression | 常用语 | 常用語 | chángyòngyǔ |

# 一

◆ 小霞的网恋 ◆
◆ 小霞的網戀 ◆

Xiǎo Xiá's Internet Romance

小霞很喜欢上网聊天儿。她觉得在网上聊天儿可以认识很多人，最近她在网上就认识了一个男朋友。小霞的父母不放心小霞在网上聊天儿，怕她遇到坏人。他们说整天上网聊天儿的人肯定不是好人，所以他们对小霞在网上认识的这个男朋友很不放心。

小霞对父母说："我也天天上网啊！难道我不是好人吗？网上有好人也有坏人。运气好的人遇到好人，运气不好的人遇到坏人。我的运气好，我碰见的这个男朋友是好人。"

小霞提出要和男朋友见面，小霞的爸爸不同意；小霞说要请男朋友来家里，小霞的妈妈不愿意。小霞觉得很委屈，她觉得爸爸妈妈一点儿都不爱她，只有她的男朋友最爱她。

自从认识这个男朋友以后，小霞就不想学习了，她整天在网上和男朋友聊天儿。小霞的父母很着急，就对小霞说："你把男朋友叫来让我们看看。他要是好人，你们可以来往；如果我们觉得他不好，你就不要再跟他聊天儿了，好好学习吧。"

小霞听了很高兴，马上给男朋友发信说："我父母要见你，你赶快来我们家吧！"平时小霞一写信，她的男朋友很快就回信，可是今天等了半天，她的男朋友也没有回信。

小霞猜想她的男朋友可能有些不好意思，就又发信说："你不要紧张，也不要害怕，我爸爸妈妈都很和气。"过了很长时间，男朋友回信了，说："小霞，对不起，我早就结婚了。"

小霞很喜歡上網聊天兒。她覺得在網上聊天兒可以認識很多人，最近她在網上就認識了一個男朋友。小霞的父母不放心小霞在網上聊天兒，怕她遇到壞人。他們說整天上網聊天兒的人肯定不是好人，所以他們對小霞在網上認識的這個男朋友很不放心。

小霞對父母說："我也天天上網啊！難道我不是好人嗎？網上有好人也有壞人。運氣好的人遇到好人，運氣不好的人遇到壞人。我的運氣好，我碰見的這個男朋友是好人。"

小霞提出要和男朋友見面，小霞的爸爸不同意；小霞說要請男朋友來家裡，小霞的媽媽不願意。小霞覺得很委屈，她覺得爸爸媽媽一點兒都不愛她，只有她的男朋友最愛她。

自從認識這個男朋友以後，小霞就不想學習了，她整天在網上和男朋友聊天兒。小霞的父母很著急，就對小霞說："你把男朋友叫來讓我們看看。他要是好人，你們可以來往；如果我們覺得他不好，你就不要再跟他聊天兒了，好好學習吧。"

小霞听了很高興，馬上給男朋友發信說："我父母要見你，你趕快來我們家吧！"平時小霞一寫信，她的男朋友很快就回信，可是今天等了半天，她的男朋友也沒有回信。

小霞猜想她的男朋友可能有些不好意思，就又發信說："你不要緊張，也不要害怕，我爸爸媽媽都很和氣。"過了很長時間，男朋友回信了，說："小霞，對不起，我早就結婚了。"

# ✦ 生词 ✦
✦ 生詞 ✦

## New Vocabulary

| | Simplified Characters | Traditional Characters | Pinyin | Part of Speech | English Definition |
|---|---|---|---|---|---|
| 1. | 网恋 | 網戀 | wǎngliàn | *n.* | Internet romance |
| 2. | 上网 | 上網 | shàngwǎng | *v.* | log onto the internet |
| 3. | 聊天儿 | 聊天兒 | liáotiānr | *v.* | chat |
| 4. | 放心 | 放心 | fàngxīn | *v.* | set one's mind at rest |
| 5. | 怕 | 怕 | pà | *v.* | be afraid of |
| 6. | 遇到 | 遇到 | yùdào | *v.* | run into; encounter |
| 7. | 坏人 | 壞人 | huàirén | *n.* | bad person |
| 8. | 整天 | 整天 | zhěngtiān | *n.* | the whole day; all day |
| 9. | 肯定 | 肯定 | kěndìng | *adv.* | certainly; definitely |
| 10. | 难道 | 難道 | nándào | *adv.* | used to reiterate a rhetorical question |
| 11. | 运气 | 運氣 | yùnqi | *n.* | good fortune; luck |
| 12. | 提出 | 提出 | tíchū | *v.* | put forward; bring up (a point) |
| 13. | 见面 | 見面 | jiànmiàn | *v.* | meet; see |
| 14. | 同意 | 同意 | tóngyì | *v.* | agree; consent |
| 15. | 愿意 | 願意 | yuànyì | *v.* | be willing; want |

| | Simplified Characters | Traditional Characters | Pinyin | Part of Speech | English Definition |
|---|---|---|---|---|---|
| 16. | 觉得 | 覺得 | juéde | *v.* | feel; think |
| 17. | 委屈 | 委屈 | wěiqu | *adj.* | feel wronged |
| 18. | 自从 | 自從 | zìcóng | *prep.* | since |
| 19. | 着急 | 著急 | zháojí | *adj.* | anxious; worry |
| 20. | 来往 | 來往 | láiwang | *v.* | contact |
| 21. | 发信 | 發信 | fāxìn | *vo.* | post a letter |
| 22. | 赶快 | 趕快 | gǎnkuài | *adj.* | at once; quickly |
| 23. | 平时 | 平時 | píngshí | *n.* | ordinary times |
| 24. | 半天 | 半天 | bàntiān | *n.* | a long time; quite a while |
| 25. | 猜想 | 猜想 | cāixiǎng | *v.* | suppose; guess |
| 26. | 不好意思 | 不好意思 | bùhǎoyìsi | *adj.* | feel embarrassed |
| 27. | 紧张 | 緊張 | jǐnzhāng | *adj.* | nervous |
| 28. | 害怕 | 害怕 | hàipà | *v.* | be scared |
| 29. | 和气 | 和氣 | héqì | *adj.* | kind; polite |
| 30. | 结婚 | 結婚 | jiéhūn | *v.* | marry; get married |

| | Simplified Characters | Traditional Characters | Pinyin | Part of Speech | English Definition |
|---|---|---|---|---|---|
| 1. | 恋爱 | 戀愛 | liàn'ài | v. | be in love; have a love affair |
| 2. | 失恋 | 失戀 | shīliàn | v. | be disappointed in a love affair |
| 3. | 热恋 | 熱戀 | rèliàn | v. | be passionately in love |
| 4. | 早恋 | 早戀 | zǎoliàn | v. | fall in love at an early age |
| 5. | 初恋 | 初戀 | chūliàn | n. | first love |
| 6. | 生死恋 | 生死戀 | shēngsǐliàn | n. | love in life or death |
| 7. | 黄昏恋 | 黃昏戀 | huánghūnliàn | n. | love between an elderly couple |
| 8. | 同性恋 | 同性戀 | tóngxìngliàn | n. | homosexual love |
| 9. | 婚外恋 | 婚外戀 | hūnwàiliàn | n. | an extramarital love affair |
| 10. | 三角恋爱 | 三角戀愛 | sānjiǎo liànài | n. | love triangle |

# 练习

## Exercises

## 一、 连接意思相近词语
Link the similar words

1. 遇到 — *nán dào*     谈话 *dàn huó* to talk
2. 从早到晚     立刻 *lì kè* at once
3. 来往     肯定 *kěn dìng* certainly
4. 聊天儿     整天
5. 马上 *mǎ shàng* immediately     碰见 *pèng jiàn* meet
6. 一定 *yī dìng* for sure     交朋友 *jiāo péng yǒu* make friends

## 二、 选择合适的词语完成句子
Choose the most appropriate phrase to complete the sentence

1. 小霞喜欢在网上聊天儿，因为
   a. 她可以不用去上学。
   b. 她可以认识很多人。
   c. 她整天没有事情做。

# 練習

## Exercises

---

## 一、連接意思相近詞語
*Link the similar words*

........................................................

| | | |
|---|---|---|
| 1. 遇到 | | 談話 |
| 2. 從早到晚 | | 立刻 |
| 3. 來往 | | 肯定 |
| 4. 聊天兒 | | 整天 |
| 5. 馬上 | | 碰見 |
| 6. 一定 | | 交朋友 |

## 二、選擇合適的詞語完成句子
*Choose the most appropriate phrase to complete the sentence*

........................................................

1. 小霞喜歡在網上聊天兒，因為
   a. 她可以不用去上學。
   b. 她可以認識很多人。
   c. 她整天沒有事情做。

2. 她父母认为 (think) rèn wéi
     ⓐ 整天上网聊天儿的人不是好人。
     b. 整天上网聊天儿的人运气不好。
     c. 整天上网聊天儿的人不爱父母。

3. 小霞的父母决定见小霞的男朋友，是为了 jué dìng (decide) shì wèi le
     a. 看看他爱不爱小霞。
     b. 看看他好看不好看。
     ⓒ 看看他是不是好人。

4. 她的男朋友没有马上给小霞回信，小霞猜想
     a. 男朋友一定很忙。
     ⓑ 男朋友不好意思。
     c. 男朋友没收到信。

三、 找出正确答案
*Choose the correct answer*

1. 为什么父母不放心小霞在网上聊天儿？
     a. 因为上网聊天儿对身体不好。
     ⓑ 因为上网聊天儿会遇到坏人。
     c. 因为上网聊天儿不能做家事。

2. 小霞为什么觉得委屈？
     a. 因为父母不让她上网去聊天儿。
     ⓑ 因为父母不让她跟男朋友见面。
     c. 因为父母不让她跟同学一起玩。

2. 她父母認為
   a. 整天上網聊天兒的人不是好人。
   b. 整天上網聊天兒的人運气不好。
   c. 整天上網聊天兒的人不愛父母。

3. 小霞的父母決定見小霞的男朋友，是為了
   a. 看看他愛不愛小霞。
   b. 看看他好看不好看。
   c. 看看他是不是好人。

4. 她的男朋友沒有馬上給小霞回信，小霞猜想
   a. 男朋友一定很忙。
   b. 男朋友不好意思。
   c. 男朋友沒收到信。

三、找出正確答案
*Choose the correct answer*

1. 為什麼父母不放心小霞在網上聊天兒？
   a. 因為上網聊天兒對身體不好。
   b. 因為上網聊天兒會遇到壞人。
   c. 因為上網聊天兒不能做家事。

2. 小霞為什麼覺得委屈？
   a. 因為父母不讓她上網去聊天兒。
   b. 因為父母不讓她跟男朋友見面。
   c. 因為父母不讓她跟同學一起玩。

3. 为什么小霞听了父母的话以后很高兴?
    ⓐ 因为父母要见小霞的男朋友。
    b. 因为父母让小霞以后多上网。
    c. 因为父母让小霞去见男朋友。

4. 小霞男朋友为什么不跟小霞父母见面?
    a. 因为他有些不好意思。
    b. 因为他没有很多时间。
    ⓒ 因为他已经有太太了。
                  wife

四、思考问题，说说你的看法

*Think about the questions and talk about your perspective*

1. 上网聊天儿有没有好处? 为什么?

2. 上网聊天儿怎样才可以不遇到坏人?

3. 你相信网上的朋友吗? 为什么?

4. 网恋好不好? 为什么?
   online date

3. 為什麼小霞听了父母的話以後很高興?
   a. 因為父母要見小霞的男朋友。
   b. 因為父母讓小霞以後多上網。
   c. 因為父母讓小霞去見男朋友。

4. 小霞男朋友為什麼不跟小霞父母見面?
   a. 因為他有些不好意思。
   b. 因為他沒有很多時間。
   c. 因為他已經有太太了。


四、思考問題，說說你的看法

*Think about the questions and talk about your perspective*

1. 上網聊天兒有沒有好處? 為什麼?

2. 上網聊天兒怎樣才可以不遇到壞人?

3. 你相信網上的朋友嗎? 為什麼?

4. 網戀好不好? 為什麼?

# 二

◆ 小丽想跟谁结婚 ◆
◆ 小麗想跟誰結婚 ◆

## Whom Should Xiǎo Lì Marry?

一个人同时跟两个人谈恋爱，这叫做三角恋爱。三角恋爱虽然不道德，但是不违法。一个人同时和两个人结婚，这叫做重婚，重婚不仅不道德，而且违法。

同时跟两个人谈恋爱是不是很幸福呢？不是。为什么呢？因为你最后只能选择跟其中一个人结婚。在你爱的两个人中间，选择跟一个人结婚，是一件很痛苦的事情。当你选择甲的时候，你会觉得乙特别好；当你选择乙的时候，你又认为甲真的不错。

那么，有没有什么好方法可以让你不痛苦呢？好像没有。不过，在中国的古书上，有个女孩子在两个男孩子中间选丈夫的故事，我们来看看她是怎么做的。

这个女孩子叫小丽，小丽很漂亮也很聪明。她左右两家邻居的男孩子一起向她求婚。左边那家的男孩子长得很英俊，但是很穷；右边那家的男孩子长得很丑，但是很富。

小丽的父母很难决定把女儿嫁给谁，就问小丽想跟谁结婚。小丽低头半天不说话。爸爸妈妈就对她说，你要是不好意思说出来的话，你就举一下手。如果你想跟左边邻居家的孩子结婚，你就举左手；如果你愿意跟右边邻居家的孩子结婚，你就举右手。

小丽想了一会儿，慢慢地举起了双手。她的父母觉得很奇怪，就问小丽：你为什么举起两只手呢？小丽回答说："我想在右边的邻居家吃饭，在左边的邻居家睡觉。"

一個人同時跟兩個人談戀愛，這叫做三角戀愛。三角戀愛雖然不道德，但是不違法。一個人同時和兩個人結婚，這叫做重婚，重婚不僅不道德，而且違法。

同時跟兩個人談戀愛是不是很幸福呢？不是。為什麼呢？因為你最後只能選擇跟其中一個人結婚。在你愛的兩個人中間，選擇跟一個人結婚，是一件很痛苦的事情。當你選擇甲的時候，你會覺得乙特別好；當你選擇乙的時候，你又認為甲真的不錯。

那麼，有沒有什麼好方法可以讓你不痛苦呢？好像沒有。不過，在中國的古書上，有個女孩子在兩個男孩子中間選丈夫的故事，我們來看看她是怎麼做的。

這個女孩子叫小麗，小麗很漂亮也很聰明。她左右兩家鄰居的男孩子一起向她求婚。左邊那家的男孩子長得很英俊，但是很窮；右邊那家的男孩子長得很醜，但是很富。

小麗的父母很難決定把女兒嫁給誰，就問小麗想跟誰結婚。小麗低頭半天不說話。爸爸媽媽就對她說，你要是不好意思說出來的話，你就舉一下手。如果你想跟左邊鄰居家的孩子結婚，你就舉左手；如果你願意跟右邊鄰居家的孩子結婚，你就舉右手。

小麗想了一會兒，慢慢地舉起了雙手。她的父母覺得很奇怪，就問小麗：你為什麼舉起兩隻手呢？小麗回答說："我想在右邊的鄰居家吃飯，在左邊的鄰居家睡覺。"

| Simplified Characters | Traditional Characters | Pinyin | Part of Speech | English Definition |
|---|---|---|---|---|
| 1. 同时 | 同時 | tóngshí | *adv.* | at the same time |
| 2. 谈恋爱 | 談戀愛 | tánliànài | *vo.* | fall in love |
| 3. 三角恋爱 | 三角戀愛 | sānjiǎo liànài | *n.* | love triangle |
| 4. 道德 | 道德 | dàodé | *n.* | morals; morality |
| 5. 违法 | 違法 | wéifǎ | *vo.* | break the law; be illegal |
| 6. 重婚 | 重婚 | chónghūn | *n.* | bigamy |
| 7. 不仅⋯ 而且 | 不僅⋯ 而且 | bùjǐn... érqiě | *conj.* | not only...but also |
| 8. 幸福 | 幸福 | xìngfú | *n./ adj.* | happiness; happy |
| 9. 选择 | 選擇 | xuǎnzé | *v.* | select; choose |
| 10. 其中 | 其中 | qízhōng | *prep.* | among (which, them) |
| 11. 痛苦 | 痛苦 | tòngkǔ | *adj.* | pain; suffering |
| 12. 当⋯时候 | 當⋯時候 | dāng... shíhou | *prep.* | when |
| 13. 甲 | 甲 | jiǎ | *n.* | first (of the ten Heavenly Stems) |

| | Simplified Characters | Traditional Characters | Pinyin | Part of Speech | English Definition |
|---|---|---|---|---|---|
| 14. | 乙 | 乙 | yǐ | *n.* | second (of the ten Heavenly Stems) |
| 15. | 特别 | 特別 | tèbié | *adv.* | especially; particularly |
| 16. | 不错 | 不錯 | bùcuò | *adj.* | not bad; pretty good |
| 17. | 古书 | 古書 | gǔshū | *n.* | ancient books |
| 18. | 左右 | 左右 | zuǒyòu | *n.* | left and right |
| 19. | 邻居 | 鄰居 | línjū | *n.* | neighbor |
| 20. | 求婚 | 求婚 | qiúhūn | *v.* | make an offer of marriage; propose |
| 21. | 英俊 | 英俊 | yīngjùn | *adj.* | handsome |
| 22. | 穷 | 窮 | qióng | *adj.* | poor; poverty-stricken |
| 23. | 丑 | 醜 | chǒu | *adj.* | ugly |
| 24. | 富 | 富 | fù | *adj.* | rich; wealthy |
| 25. | 决定 | 決定 | juédìng | *v.* | decide; decision |
| 26. | 嫁 | 嫁 | jià | *v.* | (of a woman) marry |
| 27. | 低头 | 低頭 | dītóu | *vo.* | lower (or bow, hang) one's head |
| 28. | 举手 | 舉手 | jǔshǒu | *vo.* | raise one's hand or hands |
| 29. | 双手 | 雙手 | shuāngshǒu | *n.* | both hands |
| 30. | 奇怪 | 奇怪 | qíguài | *adj.* | strange; surprising |

| | | | | |
|---|---|---|---|---|
| 常用的有关婚姻的词语 常用的有關婚姻的詞語 | | | | |
| Commonly Used Related Words and Phrases | | | | |

| | Simplified Characters | Traditional Characters | Pinyin | Part of Speech | English Definition |
|---|---|---|---|---|---|
| 1. | 婚姻 | 婚姻 | hūnyīn | *n.* | marriage; matrimony |
| 2. | 未婚 | 未婚 | wèihūn | *n.* | unmarried; single |
| 3. | 征婚 | 征婚 | zhēnghūn | *v.* | marriage seeking |
| 4. | 订婚 | 訂婚 | dìnghūn | *v.* | be engaged (to be married) |
| 5. | 赖婚 | 賴婚 | làihūn | *v.* | repudiate a marriage contract |
| 6. | 退婚 | 退婚 | tuìhūn | *v.* | break off an engagement |
| 7. | 逃婚 | 逃婚 | táohūn | *v.* | run away from wedding |
| 8. | 婚礼 | 婚禮 | hūnlǐ | *n.* | wedding ceremony |
| 9. | 已婚 | 已婚 | yǐhūn | *adj.* | married |
| 10. | 离婚 | 離婚 | líhūn | *v.* | divorce |
| 11. | 再婚 | 再婚 | zàihūn | *v.* | remarry; marry again |
| 12. | 银婚 | 銀婚 | yínhūn | *n.* | silver wedding (25th anniversary) |
| 13. | 金婚 | 金婚 | jīnhūn | *n.* | gold wedding (50th anniversary) |

| 出處 |
| --- |
| Source |

故事出處:《藝文類聚》卷四十引漢應劭《風俗通•兩袒》

　　原文: 齊人有女, 二人求之。東家子丑而富, 西家子好而貧。父母疑不能決, 問其女:"定所欲適, 難指斥言者, 偏袒令我知之。"女便兩袒, 怪問其故。云:"欲東家食, 西家宿。"此為兩袒者也。

## 一、 连接意思相反的词语
### Link the antonyms

1. 左
2. 幸福
3. 英俊
4. 结婚
5. 甲
6. 违法

丑
离婚
合法
乙
右
痛苦

## 二、 选择合适的词语完成句子
### Choose the most appropriate phrase to complete the sentence

1. 一个人同时跟两个人谈恋爱叫做
   a. 三种恋爱。
   b. 三角恋爱。
   c. 三个恋爱。

# 練習

## Exercises

### 一、連接意思相反的詞語
*Link the antonyms*

1. 左　　　　　　　醜

2. 幸福　　　　　　离婚

3. 英俊　　　　　　合法

4. 結婚　　　　　　乙

5. 甲　　　　　　　右

6. 違法　　　　　　痛苦

### 二、選擇合適的詞語完成句子
*Choose the most appropriate phrase to complete the sentence*

1. 一個人同時跟兩個人談戀愛叫做
   a. 三种戀愛。
   b. 三角戀愛。
   c. 三個戀愛。

2. 一个人同时跟两个人结婚是
    a. 两婚。
    b. 二婚。
    (c.) 重婚。

3. 小丽说，她想
    (a.) 在右边的邻居家吃饭，在左边的邻居家睡觉。
    b. 在右边的邻居家睡觉，在左边的邻居家吃饭。
    c. 在右边的邻居家吃饭，在左边的邻居家吃饭。

4. 小丽低头半天不说话，是因为
    a. 她不喜欢这两个人。
    b. 她现在还不想结婚。
    (c.) 她想嫁给这两个人。

## 三、 找出正确答案
*Choose the correct answer*

1. 为什么跟两个人同时谈恋爱最后很痛苦?
    a. 因为这两个人都不想和你结婚。
    b. 因为两个人同时可以和你结婚。
    (c.) 因为你只能选择跟一个人结婚。

2. 为什么父母很难决定把女儿嫁给谁?
    (a.) 穷孩子很英俊，富孩子很丑。
    b. 两个求婚的男孩子都很有钱。
    c. 两个求婚的男孩子都是邻居。

2. 一個人同時跟兩個人結婚是
   a. 兩婚。
   b. 二婚。
   c. 重婚。

3. 小丽說，她想
   a. 在右邊的鄰居家吃飯，在左邊的鄰居家睡覺。
   b. 在右邊的鄰居家睡覺，在左邊的鄰居家吃飯。
   c. 在右邊的鄰居家吃飯，在左邊的鄰居家吃飯。

4. 小麗低頭半天不說話，是因為
   a. 她不喜歡這兩個人。
   b. 她現在還不想結婚。
   c. 她想嫁給這兩個人。


三、 找出正確答案
*Choose the correct answer*

1. 為什麼跟兩個人同時談戀愛最後很痛苦？
   a. 因為這兩個人都不想和你結婚。
   b. 因為兩個人同時可以和你結婚。
   c. 因為你只能選擇跟一個人結婚。

2. 為什麼父母很難決定把女兒嫁給誰？
   a. 窮孩子很英俊，富孩子很醜。
   b. 兩個求婚的男孩子都很有錢。
   c. 兩個求婚的男孩子都是鄰居。

3. 父母用什么办法来决定把女儿嫁给谁？
    a. 谁先求婚就把女儿嫁给谁。
    b. 女儿喜欢谁就把她嫁给谁。
    c. 让女儿举手表示想嫁给谁。

4. 小丽想嫁给谁？
    a. 嫁给英俊的人。
    b. 嫁给他们两人。
    c. 嫁给有钱的人。

## 四、思考问题，说说你的看法

*Think about the questions and talk about your perspective*

1. 你认为小丽应该嫁给谁？为什么？

2. 嫁给有钱的人有什么好处和坏处？

3. 如果你爱的是一个穷人，你会不会跟她/他结婚？
   为什么？

4. 现在人们怎么选择要跟自己结婚的人？

3. 父母用什麼辦法來決定把女兒嫁給誰?
    a. 誰先求婚就把女兒嫁給誰。
    b. 女兒喜歡誰就把她嫁給誰。
    c. 讓女兒舉手表示想嫁給誰。

4. 小麗想嫁給誰?
    a. 嫁給英俊的人。
    b. 嫁給他們兩人。
    c. 嫁給有錢的人。

四、思考問題，說說你的看法

*Think about the questions and talk about your perspective*

1. 你認為小麗應該嫁給誰? 為什麼?

2. 嫁給有錢的人有什麼好處和壞處?

3. 如果你愛的是一個窮人，你會不會跟她/他結婚? 為什麼?

4. 現在人們怎麼選擇要跟自己結婚的人?

# 三

## ◆ 不听话的太阳 ◆
## ◆ 不聽話的太陽 ◆

### The Naughty Sun

很久以前，天上有十个太阳。太阳每天从东边走到西边，给人们带来光明，带来温暖。

那时候，上帝规定每天只能有一个太阳出来，因为如果十个太阳一起出来的话，太多的热就会给人们带来灾害。

一天，太阳们突然觉得每天只是一个太阳出去走太寂寞了，没有一点儿乐趣。于是她们就一起出去了。

当十个太阳一起出来的时候，天气就变得非常热。不一会儿，花儿热死了，树木热死了，最后连河里的水都被太阳晒干了。

人们热得受不了了，就去告诉上帝。上帝让太阳们赶快回去。可是太阳们不听上帝的话，她们在外面跑来跑去，谁也不愿意回去。

上帝看到人们都快要热死了，他很生气，于是就命令后羿把十个太阳全都杀死。

后羿是一个很有名的猎人，他射箭射得很好。后羿看到十个太阳出来害人，也非常生气，就带着弓箭爬到山上，把太阳一个一个地射了下来。

当后羿射下第九个太阳的时候，他突然想到，要是没有太阳，世界上就没有光明和温暖，那样人们也就没有办法生活了，他就留下了最后一个太阳。

后羿为人们做了一件好事情，大家都很感谢他，希望他能永远帮助人们，于是上帝就给了后羿一颗"不死药"，这颗"不死药"可以让人长生不老，永远不死。

很久以前，天上有十個太陽。太陽每天從東邊走到西邊，給人們帶來光明，帶來溫暖。

那時候，上帝規定每天只能有一個太陽出來，因為如果十個太陽一起出來的話，太多的熱就會給人們帶來災害。

一天，太陽們突然覺得每天只是一個太陽出去走太寂寞了，沒有一點兒樂趣。於是她們就一起出去了。

當十個太陽一起出來的時候，天氣就變得非常熱。不一會儿，花兒熱死了，樹木熱死了，最後連河裡的水都被太陽曬乾了。

人們熱得受不了了，就去告訴上帝。上帝讓太陽們趕快回去。可是太陽們不聽上帝的話，她們在外面跑來跑去，誰也不願意回去。

上帝看到人們都快要熱死了，他很生氣，於是就命令后羿把十個太陽全都殺死。

后羿是一個很有名的獵人，他射箭射得很好。后羿看到十個太陽出來害人，也非常生氣，就帶著弓箭爬到山上，把太陽一個一個地射了下來。

當后羿射下第九個太陽的時候，他突然想到，要是沒有太陽，世界上就沒有光明和溫暖，那樣人們也就沒有辦法生活了，他就留下了最後一個太陽。

后羿為人們做了一件好事情，大家都很感謝他，希望他能永遠幫助人們，於是上帝就給了后羿一顆“不死藥”，這顆“不死藥”可以讓人長生不老，永遠不死。

| | Simplified Characters | Traditional Characters | Pinyin | Part of Speech | English Definition |
|---|---|---|---|---|---|
| 1. | 带来 | 帶來 | dàilái | *vc.* | bring to |
| 2. | 光明 | 光明 | guāngmíng | *n.* | light; bright |
| 3. | 温暖 | 溫暖 | wēnnuǎn | *adj.* | warm |
| 4. | 上帝 | 上帝 | Shàngdì | *n.* | God |
| 5. | 规定 | 規定 | guīdìng | *v.* | rule; ordain |
| 6. | 灾害 | 災害 | zāihài | *n.* | catastrophe; disaster |
| 7. | 突然 | 突然 | tūrán | *adv.* | suddenly |
| 8. | 寂寞 | 寂寞 | jìmò | *adj.* | lonely |
| 9. | 乐趣 | 樂趣 | lèqù | *n.* | delight; pleasure; joy |
| 10. | 变得 | 變得 | biànde | *v.* | change to |
| 11. | 树木 | 樹木 | shùmù | *n.* | trees |
| 12. | 连 | 連 | lián | *conj.* | even |
| 13. | 晒干 | 曬乾 | shàigān | *vc.* | dry in the sun |
| 14. | 受不了 | 受不了 | shòubùliǎo | *vc.* | unbearable |
| 15. | 生气 | 生氣 | shēngqì | *v.* | become angry |
| 16. | 命令 | 命令 | mìnglìng | *v.* | order; command |

| | Simplified Characters | Traditional Characters | Pinyin | Part of Speech | English Definition |
|---|---|---|---|---|---|
| 17. | 后羿 | 后羿 | Hòuyì | *prn.* | person's name |
| 18. | 杀死 | 殺死 | shāsǐ | *vc.* | killed |
| 19. | 猎人 | 獵人 | lièrén | *n.* | hunter; huntsman |
| 20. | 射箭 | 射箭 | shèjiàn | *vo.* | shoot an arrow |
| 21. | 害 | 害 | hài | *v.* | injure; harm |
| 22. | 弓箭 | 弓箭 | gōngjiàn | *n.* | bow and arrow |
| 23. | 射 | 射 | shè | *v.* | shoot |
| 24. | 世界 | 世界 | shìjiè | *n.* | world |
| 25. | 留下 | 留下 | liúxià | *v.* | keep; remain |
| 26. | 为 | 為 | wèi | *prep.* | for |
| 27. | 希望 | 希望 | xīwàng | *v.* | hope; wish |
| 28. | 永远 | 永遠 | yǒngyuǎn | *adj.* | forever |
| 29. | 不死药 | 不死藥 | bùsǐyào | *n.* | immortality elixir |
| 30. | 长生不老 | 長生不老 | chángshēng bùlǎo | *id.* | immortality |

## Commonly Used Related Words and Phrases

| Simplified Characters | Traditional Characters | Pinyin | Part of Speech | English Definition |
|---|---|---|---|---|
| 1. 炎热 | 炎熱 | yánrè | *adj.* | blistering hot; sizzling |
| 2. 寒冷 | 寒冷 | hánlěng | *adj.* | cold; frigid |
| 3. 暖和 | 暖和 | nuǎnhuo | *adj.* | pleasantly warm |
| 4. 凉爽 | 涼爽 | liángshuang | *adj.* | pleasantly cool |
| 5. 干燥 | 乾燥 | gānzào | *adj.* | dry; arid |
| 6. 潮湿 | 潮濕 | cháoshī | *adj.* | moist; damp |
| 7. 晴天 | 晴天 | qíngtiān | *n.* | sunny |
| 8. 阴天 | 陰天 | yīntiān | *n.* | cloudy; overcast sky |
| 9. 下雨 | 下雨 | xiàyǔ | *v.* | rainy |
| 10. 下雪 | 下雪 | xiàxuě | *v.* | snowy |
| 11. 刮风 | 颱風 | gūafēng | *v.* | windy |
| 12. 打雷 | 打雷 | dǎléi | *v.* | thunder |
| 13. 闪电 | 閃電 | shǎndiàn | *v.* | lightning |

故事出處:《淮南子•本經訓》

　　原文:逮至堯之時,十日并出,焦禾稼,殺草木,而民無所食。猰貐、鑿齒、九嬰、大風、封稀、修蛇皆為民害。堯乃使羿誅鑿齒於疇華之野,殺九嬰於凶水之上,繳大風於青丘之澤,上射十日而下殺猰貐,斷修蛇於洞庭,禽封希於桑林。

| | 练习 |
|---|---|
| | Exercises |

## 一、 连接意思相近的词语
*Link the similar words*

....................................................................................

1. 长生不老      很短时间

2. 受不了了      东跑西跑

3. 不一会儿      太寂寞了

4. 带来灾害      永远不死

5. 没有乐趣      不能忍受

6. 跑来跑去      带来不幸

## 二、 选择合适的词语完成句子
*Choose the most appropriate phrase to complete the sentence*

....................................................................................

1. 每天只有一个太阳出来，是因为
     a. 其它的太阳都要睡觉。
     b. 太阳太多会带来灾害。
     c. 不要很多光明和温暖。

| | |
|---|---|
| 練習 | |
| Exercises | |

## 一、 連接意思相近的詞語
Link the similar words

1. 長生不老　　　　很短時間

2. 受不了了　　　　東跑西跑

3. 不一會儿　　　　太寂寞了

4. 帶來災害　　　　永遠不死

5. 沒有樂趣　　　　不能忍受

6. 跑來跑去　　　　帶來不幸

## 二、 選擇合適的詞語完成句子
Choose the most appropriate phrase to complete the sentence

1. 每天只有一個太陽出來，是因為
  a. 其它的太陽都要睡覺。
  b. 太陽太多會帶來災害。
  c. 不要很多光明和溫暖。

2. 十个太阳一起出来，结果
    a. 人们高兴得不得了。
    b. 人们都不再寂寞了。
    c. 人们热得都受不了。

3. 上帝非常生气，因为
    a. 人们都快要热死了。
    b. 光明和温暖太多了。
    c. 一个太阳太寂寞了。

4. 后羿留了一个太阳，是因为
    a. 他忘记了上帝的命令。
    b. 他喜欢最后这个太阳。
    c. 他要留下光明和温暖。

## 三、找出正确答案
*Choose the correct answer*

1. 太阳们为什么要一起出来？
    a. 太阳们要给人们带来灾害。
    b. 人们希望太阳们一起出来。
    c. 太阳觉得出来一个太寂寞。

2. 后羿为什么要杀死太阳？
    a. 上帝命令他把太阳杀死。
    b. 人们不需要光明和温暖。
    c. 可以得到一颗"不死药"。

2. 十個太陽一起出來，結果
    a. 人們高興得不得了。
    b. 人們都不再寂寞了。
    c. 人們熱得都受不了。

3. 上帝非常生氣，因為
    a. 人們都快要熱死了。
    b. 光明和溫暖太多了。
    c. 一個太陽太寂寞了。

4. 后羿留了一個太陽，是因為
    a. 他忘記了上帝的命令。
    b. 他喜歡最後這個太陽。
    c. 他要留下光明和溫暖。

三、找出正確答案

*Choose the correct answer*

1. 太陽們為什麼要一起出來？
    a. 太陽們要給人們帶來災害。
    b. 人們希望太陽們一起出來。
    c. 太陽覺得出來一個太寂寞。

2. 后羿為什麼要殺死太陽？
    a. 上帝命令他把太陽殺死。
    b. 人們不需要光明和溫暖。
    c. 可以得到一顆"不死藥"。

3. 为什么天气变得非常热？
   a. 很久很久没有下雨了。
   b. 十个太阳一起出来了。
   c. 太阳都不愿意出来了。

4. 上帝为什么给后羿一颗"不死药"？
   a. 希望他下次再射太阳。
   b. 希望他做一个好猎人。
   c. 希望他永远帮助人们。

四、思考问题，说说你的看法
*Think about the questions and talk about your perspective*

1. 太阳们一起出来是想要给人们带来灾害吗？

2. 太阳们为什么不听上帝的话？

3. 后羿应该杀死九个太阳吗？为什么？

4. 如果一个人只想到自己，会给别人带来什么？

3. 為什麼天氣變得非常熱?
    a. 很久很久沒有下雨了。
    b. 十個太陽一起出來了。
    c. 太陽都不願意出來了。

4. 上帝為什麼給后羿一顆 "不死藥" ?
    a. 希望他下次再射太陽。
    b. 希望他做一個好獵人。
    c. 希望他永遠幫助人們。


四、思考問題，說說你的看法

*Think about the questions and talk about your perspective*

1. 太陽們一起出來是想要給人們帶來災害嗎?

2. 太陽們為什麼不听上帝的話?

3. 后羿應該殺死九個太陽嗎? 為什麼?

4. 如果一個人只想到自己，會給別人帶來什麼?

# 四

♦ 月宫里的嫦娥 ♦
♦ 月宫裡的嫦娥 ♦

## The Moon Palace's Cháng'é

后羿的妻子叫嫦娥，嫦娥长得又漂亮又聪明。嫦娥知道上帝给了后羿一颗"不死药"，她心想：人永远活着多好啊！谁愿意死呢？！

一天，嫦娥趁后羿不在家的时候，偷偷地把那颗"不死药"吃了下去。嫦娥把药吃下去以后，突然发觉自己的身体变轻了，而且越来越轻。渐渐地嫦娥升到了天空中，飞到了月亮上。这时候嫦娥才明白，"不死药"原来是让人永远活在天上的。

嫦娥飞到月亮上以后，就住在月宫里。月宫很大，也很漂亮。月宫的院子里有一棵高大的桂花树，树底下还有一只可爱的小白兔。嫦娥每天什么事情都不做，只是唱歌，跳舞。

过了一段时间以后，嫦娥就觉得没有意思了。月宫虽然很大，可是没有人跟她一起住；这里虽然有香甜的桂花酒，可是没有人跟她一起喝。月亮上没有人和她说话，没有人听她唱歌，也没有人跟她跳舞，嫦娥一个人感到很寂寞。

这时候，她想起了她的丈夫后羿，想起了以前的邻居，想起了许多好朋友。嫦娥心里很难过，她后悔自己偷吃了"不死药"。

一年又一年，很多年过去了，嫦娥一个人呆在冷冰冰的月宫里。她常常在想：每当月亮圆的时候，人们就望着月亮，望着月宫里的我。很多人羡慕我，都以为我很快乐，我很幸福。

其实，我是一个很可怜的人。我不想呆在月亮上了，我要回到人间去。现在如果有一颗药能让我回去，我一定……。

后羿的妻子叫嫦娥，嫦娥長得又漂亮又聰明。嫦娥知道上帝給了后羿一顆"不死藥"，她心想：人永遠活著多好啊！誰願意死呢？！

一天，嫦娥趁后羿不在家的時候，偷偷地把那顆"不死藥"吃了下去。嫦娥把藥吃下去以後，突然發覺自己的身体變輕了，而且越來越輕。漸漸地嫦娥昇到了天空中，飛到了月亮上。這時候嫦娥才明白，"不死藥"原來是讓人永遠活在天上的。

嫦娥飛到月亮上以後，就住在月宮裡。月宮很大，也很漂亮。月宮的院子裡有一棵高大的桂花樹，樹底下還有一只可愛的小白兔。嫦娥每天什麼事情都不做，只是唱歌，跳舞。

過了一段時間以後，嫦娥就覺得沒有意思了。月宮雖然很大，可是沒有人跟她一起住；這裡雖然有香甜的桂花酒，可是沒有人跟她一起喝。月亮上沒有人和她說話，沒有人聽她唱歌，也沒有人跟她跳舞，嫦娥一個人感到很寂寞。

這時候，她想起了她的丈夫后羿，想起了以前的鄰居，想起了許多好朋友。嫦娥心里很難過，她後悔自己偷吃了"不死藥"。

一年又一年，很多年過去了，嫦娥一個人呆在冷冰冰的月宮裡。她常常在想：每當月亮圓的時候，人們就望著月亮，望著月宮裡的我。很多人羨慕我，都以為我很快樂，我很幸福。

其實，我是一個很可憐的人。我不想呆在月亮上了，我要回到人間去。現在如果有一顆藥能讓我回去，我一定……。

| | Simplified Characters | Traditional Characters | Pinyin | Part of Speech | English Definition |
|---|---|---|---|---|---|
| 1. | 月宫 | 月宫 | yuègōng | *n.* | the palace of the moon |
| 2. | 嫦娥 | 嫦娥 | Cháng'é | *prn.* | the goddess of the moon |
| 3. | 妻子 | 妻子 | qīzi | *n.* | wife |
| 4. | 趁 | 趁 | chèn | *prep.* | take advantage of (an opportunity) |
| 5. | 偷偷地 | 偷偷地 | tōutōude | *adv.* | stealthily |
| 6. | 发觉 | 發覺 | fājué | *v.* | find; detect |
| 7. | 身体 | 身體 | shēntǐ | *n.* | body |
| 8. | 轻 | 輕 | qīng | *adj.* | light |
| 9. | 渐渐地 | 漸漸地 | jiànjiànde | *adv.* | gradually; little by little |
| 10. | 升 | 昇 | shēng | *v.* | rise into |
| 11. | 天空 | 天空 | tiānkōng | *n.* | the sky |
| 12. | 院子 | 院子 | yuànzi | *n.* | yard |
| 13. | 桂花树 | 桂花樹 | guìhuāshù | *n.* | sweet-scented osmanthus bush |
| 14. | 兔 | 兔 | tù | *n.* | rabbit |
| 15. | 可爱 | 可愛 | kě ài | *adj.* | lovable; lovely |

| | Simplified Characters | Traditional Characters | Pinyin | Part of Speech | English Definition |
|---|---|---|---|---|---|
| 16. | 香甜 | 香甜 | xiāngtián | *adj.* | fragrant and sweet |
| 17. | 酒 | 酒 | jiǔ | *n.* | wine |
| 18. | 丈夫 | 丈夫 | zhàngfu | *n.* | husband |
| 19. | 原先 | 原先 | yuánxiān | *adv.* | original |
| 20. | 难过 | 難過 | nánguò | *adj.* | sad; feel badly |
| 21. | 后悔 | 後悔 | hòuhuǐ | *v.* | regret; repent |
| 22. | 呆 | 呆 | dāi | *v.* | stay |
| 23. | 冷冰冰 | 冷冰冰 | lěngbīngbīng | *adj.* | ice-cold |
| 24. | 望 | 望 | wàng | *v.* | gaze into the distance |
| 25. | 羡慕 | 羨慕 | xiànmù | *v.* | to admire; to envy |
| 26. | 以为 | 以為 | yǐwéi | *v.* | think; believe (mistakenly) |
| 27. | 快乐 | 快樂 | kuài lè | *adj.* | happy; joyful |
| 28. | 其实 | 其實 | qíshí | *adv.* | actually; in fact |
| 29. | 可怜 | 可憐 | kě lián | *adj.* | pitiful |
| 30. | 人间 | 人間 | rénjiān | *n.* | human world |

◆ 常用的有关天体的词语 ◆
◆ 常用的有關天體的詞語 ◆

# Commonly Used Related Words and Phrases

| | Simplified Characters | Traditional Characters | Pinyin | Part of Speech | English Definition |
|---|---|---|---|---|---|
| 1. | 宇宙 | 宇宙 | yǔzhòu | *n.* | universe; cosmos |
| 2. | 月球 | 月球 | yuèqiú | *n.* | the moon |
| 3. | 星星 | 星星 | xīngxīng | *n.* | star |
| 4. | 流星 | 流星 | liúxīng | *n.* | meteor; shooting star |
| 5. | 陨星 | 隕星 | yǔnxīng | *n.* | meteorite |
| 6. | 卫星 | 衛星 | wèixīng | *n.* | satellite; moon; artificial satellite |
| 7. | 北斗星 | 北斗星 | běidǒuxīng | *n.* | the Big Dipper |
| 8. | 银河 | 銀河 | yínhé | *n.* | the Milky Way |
| 9. | 日食 | 日食 | rìshí | *n.* | solar eclipse |
| 10. | 月食 | 月食 | yuèshí | *n.* | lunar eclipse |
| 11. | 月牙 | 月牙 | yuèyá | *n.* | crescent moon |
| 12. | 地球 | 地球 | dìqiú | *n.* | the earth; the globe |

| 出處 |
|:---:|
| Source |

故事出處：《淮南子•覽冥訓》

　　原文：羿請不死藥於西王母，姮娥竊以奔月，悵然有喪，無以續之。

| | |
|:---:|:---:|
| 练习 | |
| Exercises | |

## 一、 连接意思相反的词语
*Link the antonyms*

1. 漂亮         温暖

2. 突然         难吃

3. 冰冷         难过

4. 人间         难看

5. 快乐         渐渐地

6. 香甜         天上

## 二、 选择合适的词语完成句子
*Choose the most appropriate phrase to complete the sentence*

1. 嫦娥偷偷地把 "不死药" 吃了下去，她是想
        a. 离开丈夫后羿。
        b. 飞到月亮上去。
        c. 永远活在人间。

一、 連接意思相反的詞語
*Link the antonyms*

1. 漂亮　　　　　溫暖

2. 突然　　　　　難吃

3. 冰冷　　　　　難過

4. 人間　　　　　難看

5. 快樂　　　　　漸漸地

6. 香甜　　　　　天上

二、 選擇合適的詞語完成句子
*Choose the most appropriate phrase to complete the sentence*

1. 嫦娥偷偷地把 "不死藥" 吃了下去, 她是想
　　a. 離開丈夫后羿。
　　b. 飛到月亮上去。
　　c. 永遠活在人間。

2. 嫦娥飞到月亮上以后很后悔，是因为
    a. 她不喜欢小白兔。
    b. 在月宫里很寂寞。
    c. 不喜欢喝桂花酒。

3. 嫦娥是一个可怜的人，是因为
    a. 她的丈夫离开了她。
    b. 她在月宫里非常忙。
    c. 她没有邻居和朋友。

4. 很多人羡慕嫦娥，是因为
    a. 嫦娥又幸福又快乐。
    b. 嫦娥又漂亮又聪明。
    c. 嫦娥有许多好朋友。

## 三、找出正确答案

*Choose the correct answer*

1. "不死药"的作用是什么？
    a. 让人永远在天空中飞。
    b. 让人能永远活在天上。
    c. 让人能永远活在人间。

2. 为什么嫦娥在月宫里只是唱歌跳舞？
    a. 因为月宫里有桂花树和小白兔。
    b. 因为月宫太大，太漂亮了。
    c. 因为月宫里没有事情可以做。

2. 嫦娥飛到月亮上以後很後悔，是因為
　　a. 她不喜歡小白兔。
　　b. 在月宮裡很寂寞。
　　c. 不喜歡喝桂花酒。

3. 嫦娥是一個可憐的人，是因為
　　a. 她的丈夫离開了她。
　　b. 她在月宮裡非常忙。
　　c. 她沒有鄰居和朋友。

4. 很多人羨慕嫦娥，是因為
　　a. 嫦娥又幸福又快樂。
　　b. 嫦娥又漂亮又聰明。
　　c. 嫦娥有許多好朋友。

# 三、找出正確答案
*Choose the correct answer*

1. "不死藥"的作用是什麼？
　　a. 讓人永遠在天空中飛。
　　b. 讓人能永遠活在天上。
　　c. 讓人能永遠活在人間。

2. 為什麼嫦娥在月宮裡只是唱歌跳舞？
　　a. 因為月宮裡有桂花樹和小白兔。
　　b. 因為月宮太大，太漂亮了。
　　c. 因為月宮裡沒有事情可以做。

3. 月宫里有什么？
   a. 有许多桂花树和许多小白兔。
   b. 有一棵桂花树和一只小白兔。
   c. 有许多新邻居和许多好朋友。

4. 嫦娥是什么时候偷吃了"不死药"的？
   a. 后羿不在家的时候。
   b. 没有事情做的时候。
   c. 后羿给她不死药的时候。

## 四、思考问题，说说你的看法
Think about the questions and talk about your perspective

........................................................................................

1. 你觉得嫦娥是不是一个可怜的人？为什么？

2. 你认为人是不是都愿意永远活着？为什么？

3. 一个人怎么做才不会后悔？

4. 一个人的时候为什么会感到寂寞？

3. 月宮裡有什麼？
    a. 有許多桂花樹和許多小白兔。
    b. 有一棵桂花樹和一只小白兔。
    c. 有許多新鄰居和許多好朋友。

4. 嫦娥是什麼時候偷吃了"不死藥"的？
    a. 后羿不在家的時候。
    b. 沒有事情做的時候。
    c. 后羿給她不死藥的時候。

四、思考問題，說說你的看法

*Think about the questions and talk about your perspective*

1. 你覺得嫦娥是不是一個可憐的人？為什麼？

2. 你認為人是不是都愿意永遠活著？為什麼？

3. 一個人怎麼做才不會后悔？

4. 一個人的時候為什麼會感到寂寞？

# 五

◆ 喜欢吃中国菜 ◆
◆ 喜歡吃中國菜 ◆

Enjoying Chinese Food

外国人喜欢吃中国菜，他们说中国菜又好吃又便宜。在(外国人)看来，不管是上海饭馆还是四川餐厅，中国菜的味道差不多都一样。其实，中国不同地方的菜有不同的味道。比如上海菜比较甜，陕西菜比较咸，四川菜比较辣，山西菜比较酸。

中国菜很早就随着中国移民来到海外了。那时海外的中国人比较少，到中国饭馆吃饭的大都是外国人，中国饭馆为了适应外国人的口味就改变一些菜的味道，结果许多中国饭馆的菜不再是地道的中国菜了，而且不管是上海饭馆，还是四川餐厅，菜的味道都差不多一样。

现在海外的中国人多起来了，有些中国饭馆就做出了味道和样式完全不同的两种菜，准备了两种不同的菜单。他们给中国人吃的是地道的中国菜，给外国人吃的是洋化了的中国菜。

外国人知道中国人吃饭用筷子，于是他们吃中国饭时也用筷子。其实，中国人很早以前也是用刀叉吃饭的，只是后来人们觉得刀叉是武器，在饭桌上看起来不文明，才改用筷子的。

中国人吃饭会发出一些呼噜呼噜的响声，特别是吃面条和喝稀饭的时候，人们觉得吃饭有呼噜呼噜的响声才表明饭菜做得好吃。

中国人吃饭可以发出响声，但是吃饭的时候不许说话，孔子三千年以前就说过："食不语，寝不言"，意思是说吃饭和睡觉的时候都不许说话。可是不知道为什么，在中国餐馆你常常可以看到许多人坐在饭桌前，一边儿吃饭，一边儿大声说话。

**外**國人喜歡吃中國菜，他們說中國菜又好吃又便宜。在外國人看來，不管是上海飯館還是四川餐廳，中國菜的味道差不多都一樣。其實，中國不同地方的菜有不同的味道。比如上海菜比較甜，陝西菜比較鹹，四川菜比較辣，山西菜比較酸。

中國菜很早就隨著中國移民來到海外了。那時海外的中國人比較少，到中國飯館吃飯的大都是外國人，中國飯館為了適應外國人的口味就改變一些菜的味道，結果許多中國飯館的菜不再是地道的中國菜了，而且不管是上海飯館，還是四川餐廳，菜的味道都差不多一樣。

現在海外的中國人多起來了，有些中國飯館就做出了味道和樣式完全不同的兩种菜，準備了兩種不同的菜單。他們給中國人吃的是地道的中國菜，給外國人吃的是洋化了的中國菜。

外國人知道中國人吃飯用筷子，於是他們吃中國飯時也用筷子。其實，中國人很早以前也是用刀叉吃飯的，只是後來人們覺得刀叉是武器，在飯桌上看起來不文明，才改用筷子的。

中國人吃飯會發出一些呼嚕呼嚕的響聲，特別是吃麵條和喝稀飯的時候，人們覺得吃飯有呼嚕呼嚕的響聲才表明飯菜做得好吃。

中國人吃飯可以發出響聲，但是吃飯的時候不許說話，孔子三千年以前就說過："食不語，寢不言"，意思是說吃飯和睡覺的時候都不許說話。可是不知道為什麼，在中國餐館你常常可以看到許多人坐在飯桌前，一邊兒吃飯，一邊兒大聲說話。

# ✦ 生词 ✦
## ✦ 生詞 ✦

### New Vocabulary

| | Simplified Characters | Traditional Characters | Pinyin | Part of Speech | English Definition |
|---|---|---|---|---|---|
| 1. | 便宜 | 便宜 | piányi | *adj.* | cheap; inexpensive |
| 2. | 味道 | 味道 | wèidào | *n.* | taste; flavor |
| 3. | 比较 | 比較 | bǐjiào | *adv.* | comparatively |
| 4. | 甜 | 甜 | tián | *adj.* | sweet |
| 5. | 咸 | 鹹 | xián | *adj.* | salty; salted |
| 6. | 辣 | 辣 | là | *adj.* | hot (of taste); burn |
| 7. | 酸 | 酸 | suān | *n.* | sour |
| 8. | 随着 | 隨著 | suízhe | *v.* | follow |
| 9. | 移民 | 移民 | yímín | *n.* | emigrant; immigrant |
| 10. | 海外 | 海外 | hǎiwài | *n.* | overseas; abroad |
| 11. | 适应 | 適應 | shìyìng | *v.* | accommodate |
| 12. | 口味 | 口味 | kǒuwèi | *n.* | a person's taste (for food) |
| 13. | 地道 | 地道 | dìdào | *adj.* | authentic; genuine |
| 14. | 样式 | 樣式 | yàngshì | *n.* | style |
| 15. | 菜单 | 菜單 | càidān | *n.* | menu |

| | Simplified Characters | Traditional Characters | Pinyin | Part of Speech | English Definition |
|---|---|---|---|---|---|
| 16. | 洋化 | 洋化 | yánghuà | v. | Westernized |
| 17. | 刀叉 | 刀叉 | dāochā | n. | knife and fork |
| 18. | 武器 | 武器 | wǔqì | n. | weapon |
| 19. | 文明 | 文明 | wénmíng | n. | civilization |
| 20. | 改用 | 改用 | gǎiyòng | v. | change to use |
| 21. | 发出响声 | 發出響聲 | fāchūxiǎng shēng | vo. | emit a sound |
| 22. | 面条 | 麵條 | miàntiáo | n. | noodles |
| 23. | 稀饭 | 稀飯 | xīfàn | n. | rice soup |
| 24. | 呼噜 | 呼嚕 | hūlū | n. | slurping sound |
| 25. | 表明 | 表明 | biǎomíng | v. | make known; indicate |
| 26. | 许 | 許 | xǔ | v. | allow; permit |
| 27. | 食 | 食 | shí | v./n. | eat; food |
| 28. | 语 | 語 | yǔ | v. | talk; speak |
| 29. | 寝 | 寢 | qǐn | v. | sleep |
| 30. | 言 | 言 | yán | v. | talk; speak |

◆ 常用的有关中国饭菜的词语 ◆
◆ 常用的有關中國飯菜的詞語 ◆

## Commonly Used Related Words and Phrases

| | Simplified Characters | Traditional Characters | Pinyin | Part of Speech | English Definition |
|---|---|---|---|---|---|
| 1. | 米饭 | 米飯 | mǐfàn | *n.* | rice |
| 2. | 馒头 | 饅頭 | mántou | *n.* | steamed bun |
| 3. | 包子 | 包子 | bāozi | *n.* | steamed stuffed bun |
| 4. | 饺子 | 餃子 | jiǎozi | *n.* | dumpling (with stuffing) |
| 5. | 锅贴 | 鍋貼 | guōtiē | *n.* | fried dumpling |
| 6. | 馄饨 | 餛飩 | húntun | *n.* | dumpling soup |
| 7. | 葱油饼 | 蔥油餅 | cōngyóubǐng | *n.* | scallion pancake |
| 8. | 汤 | 湯 | tāng | *n.* | soup |
| 9. | 油条 | 油條 | yóutiāo | *n.* | deep-fried twisted dough sticks |
| 10. | 豆浆 | 豆漿 | dòujiāng | *n.* | soy milk |
| 11. | 方便面 | 方便麵 | fāngbiànmiàn | *n.* | instant noodles |
| 12. | 面包 | 麵包 | miànbāo | *n.* | bread |

| 出處 |
| --- |
| Source |

詞語出處:《論語•鄉党》
　　原文:食不語,寢不言。

## 一、 连接意思相关的词语
*Link the related words*

........................................................................

1. 餐馆          稀饭

2. 筷子          咸辣

3. 地道          饭馆

4. 面条          四川

5. 甜酸          刀叉

6. 上海          洋化

## 二、 选择合适的词语完成句子
*Choose the most appropriate phrase to complete the sentence*

........................................................................

1. 外国人喜欢吃中国菜，因为
     a. 中国菜甜、酸、咸、辣。
     b. 中国菜有不同的味道。
     c. 中国菜又好吃又便宜。

# 練習

## Exercises

---

## 一、連接意思相關的詞語
*Link the related words*

........................................................

1. 餐馆          稀飯

2. 筷子          咸辣

3. 地道          飯館

4. 面條          四川

5. 甜酸          刀叉

6. 上海          洋化

## 二、選擇合適的詞語完成句子
*Choose the most appropriate phrase to complete the sentence*

........................................................

1. 外國人喜歡吃中國菜，因為
   a. 中國菜甜、酸、咸、辣。
   b. 中國菜有不同的味道。
   c. 中國菜又好吃又便宜。

2. 中国饭馆改变中国菜的味道，是
    a. 为了让菜的味道都一样。
    b. 为了适应外国人的口味。
    c. 为了让中国菜又辣又酸。

3 现在中国人吃饭用筷子，其实很早以前
    a. 中国人吃饭用刀叉。
    b. 中国人吃饭用筷子。
    c. 外国人吃饭用筷子。

4. 中国人吃饭的时候
    a. 可以说话。
    b. 可以发出响声。
    c. 可以说话也可以发出响声。

## 三、找出正确答案

*Choose the correct answer*

1. 在中国陕西菜和山西菜有什么不同？
    a. 山西菜酸，陕西菜咸。
    b. 陕西菜辣，山西菜酸。
    c. 山西菜酸，陕西菜甜。

2. 为什么中国人吃饭用筷子不用刀叉？
    a. 中国人觉得筷子很便宜。
    b. 中国人很不习惯用刀叉。
    c. 中国人觉得刀叉是武器。

2. 中國飯館改變中國菜的味道，是
   a. 為了讓菜的味道都一樣。
   b. 為了适應外國人的口味。
   c. 為了讓中國菜又辣又酸。

3. 現在中國人吃飯用筷子，其實很早以前
   a. 中國人吃飯用刀叉。
   b. 中國人吃飯用筷子。
   c. 外國人吃飯用筷子。

4. 中國人吃飯的時候
   a. 可以說話。
   b. 可以發出響聲。
   c. 可以說話也可以發出響聲。

## 三、找出正確答案
*Choose the correct answer*

1. 在中國陝西菜和山西菜有什麼不同？
   a. 山西菜酸，陝西菜咸。
   b. 陝西菜辣，山西菜酸。
   c. 山西菜酸，陝西菜甜。

2. 為什麼中國人吃飯用筷子不用刀叉？
   a. 中國人覺得筷子很便宜。
   b. 中國人很不習慣用刀叉。
   c. 中國人覺得刀叉是武器。

3. 为什么中国人吃饭可以发出声音?
   a. 发出声音表示饭菜又辣又咸。
   b. 发出声音表示饭菜做得好吃。
   c. 发出声音表示吃饭的人很饿。

4. 为什么海外中国饭馆准备地道的中国菜和洋化的中国菜?
   a. 地道的中国菜又好吃又便宜。
   b. 适合中国人和外国人的口味。
   c. 外国人喜欢吃两种不同的菜。

## 四、思考问题，说说你的看法
*Think about the questions and talk about your perspective*

1. 你在家吃饭的时候可以发出声音吗? 可以说话吗?
   为什么?

2. 你认为中国饭馆应不应该准备两种不同的菜单?
   为什么?

3. 你觉得用筷子和用刀叉吃饭各有什么好处?

4. 在中国的西方饭馆应不应该改变菜的味道来适应中国
   人的口味?

3. 為什麼中國人吃飯可以發出聲音？
    a. 發出聲音表示飯菜又辣又咸。
    b. 發出聲音表示飯菜做得好吃。
    c. 發出聲音表示吃飯的人很餓。

4. 為什麼海外中國飯館准備地道的中國菜和洋化的中國菜？
    a. 地道的中國菜又好吃又便宜。
    b. 適合中國人和外國人的口味。
    c. 外國人喜歡吃兩種不同的菜。


四、思考問題，說說你的看法

*Think about the questions and talk about your perspective*

1. 你在家吃飯的時候可以發出聲音嗎？可以說話嗎？為什麼？

2. 你認為中國飯館應不應該准備兩种不同的菜單？為什麼？

3. 你覺得用筷子和用刀叉吃飯各有什麼好處？

4. 在中國的西方飯館應不應該改變菜的味道來適應中國人的口味？

# 六

◆ 中国画儿里有意思 ◆
◆ 中國畫儿裡有意思 ◆

## Chinese Paintings and Their Meanings

只要有中国人的地方就有中国画儿。中国人特别喜欢中国画儿，这是因为中国画儿不仅好看，而且画儿里面的花啊、鸟啊、树啊、人物啊什么的，都有一些特殊的含义。

例如：人们喜欢画着许多大牡丹花的画儿，这幅画儿叫做"荣华富贵"。中国人认为牡丹花代表着大福大贵，人们喜欢牡丹花，就是希望自己今后也能大福大贵。

老人们都喜欢画着松树和仙鹤的画儿，这幅画儿叫做"松鹤延年"。松树和仙鹤可以活很长时间，"松鹤延年"意思是祝愿老人像松树和仙鹤那样健康、长寿。

新婚夫妇的家里大都挂有鸳鸯游水的画儿，这幅画儿的意思是说夫妻两人要像鸳鸯那样白头到老。据说一对鸳鸯到老都不会分离的。

如果一幅画儿上画着两只喜鹊飞到家门口，这幅画儿就叫做"双喜临门"。从古到今，所有的中国人都喜欢喜鹊，就是因为喜鹊的"喜"字和喜事的"喜"字是同一个字，"双喜临门"这幅画儿的意思是说两件喜事一起来到家里了。

有时候你也会觉得很奇怪，一幅漂亮的画儿上面怎么会有几只很难看的蝙蝠呢？原来蝙蝠的"蝠"和福气的"福"读音一样，画儿上有了蝙蝠，意思是说你的福气就要到了。

中国画儿表达了人们美好的希望和祝愿。现在不但中国人喜欢中国画儿，就连外国人也都喜欢又好看又有深刻含义的中国画儿了。

只要有中國人的地方就有中國畫兒。中國人特別喜歡中國畫兒，這是因為中國畫兒不僅好看，而且畫兒裡面的花啊、鳥啊、樹啊、人物啊什麼的，都有一些特殊的含義。

例如：人們喜歡畫著許多大牡丹花的畫兒，這幅畫兒叫做"榮華富貴"。中國人認為牡丹花代表著大福大貴，人們喜歡牡丹花，就是希望自己今後也能大福大貴。

老人們都喜歡畫著松樹和仙鶴的畫兒，這幅畫兒叫做"松鶴延年"。松樹和仙鶴可以活很長時間，"松鶴延年"意思是祝願老人像松樹和仙鶴那樣健康、長壽。

新婚夫婦的家裡大都挂有鴛鴦游水的畫兒，這幅畫兒的意思是說夫妻兩人要像鴛鴦那樣白頭到老。據說一對鴛鴦到老都不會分離的。

如果一幅畫兒上畫著兩隻喜鵲飛到家門口，這幅畫兒就叫做"雙喜臨門"。從古到今，所有的中國人都喜歡喜鵲，就是因為喜鵲的"喜"字和喜事的"喜"字是同一個字，"雙喜臨門"這幅畫兒的意思是說兩件喜事一起來到家裡了。

有時候你也會覺得很奇怪，一幅漂亮的畫兒上面怎麼會有幾隻很難看的蝙蝠呢？原來蝙蝠的"蝠"和福气的"福"讀音一樣，畫兒上有了蝙蝠，意思是說你的福氣就要到了。

中國畫兒表達了人們美好的希望和祝願。現在不但中國人喜歡中國畫兒，就連外國人也都喜歡又好看又有深刻含義的中國畫兒了。

| | Simplified Characters | Traditional Characters | Pinyin | Part of Speech | English Definition |
|---|---|---|---|---|---|
| 1. | 只要…就 | 只要…就 | zhǐyào…jiù | *conj.* | if only; as long as |
| 2. | 含义 | 含義 | hányì | *n.* | meaning; implication |
| 3. | 特殊 | 特殊 | tèshū | *adj.* | special |
| 4. | 人物 | 人物 | rénwù | *n.* | figure |
| 5. | 牡丹花 | 牡丹花 | mǔdanhuā | *n.* | peony flower |
| 6. | 幅 | 幅 | fú | *m.* | classifier; measure word |
| 7. | 荣华富贵 | 榮華富貴 | rónghuá fùguì | *id.* | high rank and great wealth |
| 8. | 认为 | 認為 | rènwéi | *v.* | think; consider |
| 9. | 代表 | 代表 | dàibiǎo | *v.* | represent |
| 10. | 大福大贵 | 大福大貴 | dàfúdàguì | *adj* | good fortune and high rank |
| 11. | 松树 | 松樹 | sōngshù | *n.* | pine tree |
| 12. | 仙鹤 | 仙鶴 | xiānhè | *n.* | red-crowned crane |
| 13. | 松鹤延年 | 松鶴延年 | sōnghè yánnián | *id.* | pine and crane (symbols of longevity) |

| | Simplified Characters | Traditional Characters | Pinyin | Part of Speech | English Definition |
|---|---|---|---|---|---|
| 14. | 祝愿 | 祝愿 | zhùyuàn | *v.* | wish |
| 15. | 健康 | 健康 | jiànkāng | *adj.* | health |
| 16. | 长寿 | 長壽 | chángshòu | *adj* | long life |
| 17. | 挂 | 掛 | guà | *v.* | hang |
| 18. | 鸳鸯 | 鴛鴦 | yuānyang | *n.* | Mandarin duck |
| 19. | 夫妻 | 夫妻 | fūqī | *n.* | husband and wife |
| 20. | 白头到老 | 白頭到老 | báitóu dàolǎo | *id.* | to live together until old age |
| 21. | 据说 | 據說 | jùshuō | *prep.* | it is said; they say |
| 22. | 一对 | 一對 | yī duì | *m.* | a couple |
| 23. | 分离 | 分離 | fēnlí | *v.* | separate; sever |
| 24. | 喜鹊 | 喜鵲 | xǐquè | *n.* | magpie |
| 25. | 双喜临门 | 雙喜臨門 | shuāngxǐ línmén | *id.* | a double blessing has descended upon the house |
| 26. | 蝙蝠 | 蝙蝠 | biānfú | *n.* | bat |
| 27. | 福气 | 福氣 | fúqi | *n.* | good fortune |
| 28. | 读音 | 讀音 | dúyīn | *n.* | pronunciation |
| 29. | 表达 | 表達 | biǎodá | *v.* | express; convey |
| 30. | 深刻 | 深刻 | shēnkè | *adj.* | deep; profound |

## Commonly Used Related Words and Phrases

| Simplified Characters | Traditional Characters | Pinyin | Part of Speech | English Definition |
|---|---|---|---|---|
| 1. 中国画 | 中國畫 | Zhōngguóhuà | *n.* | Chinese painting |
| 2. 山水画 | 山水畫 | shānshuǐhuà | *n.* | landscape painting |
| 3. 花鸟画 | 花鳥畫 | huāniǎohuà | *n.* | painting of flowers and birds |
| 4. 人物画 | 人物畫 | rénwùhuà | *n.* | figure painting |
| 5. 水彩画 | 水彩畫 | shuǐcǎihuà | *n.* | watercolor |
| 6. 水墨画 | 水墨畫 | shuǐmòhuà | *n.* | ink and water painting |
| 7. 风景画 | 風景畫 | fēngjǐnghuà | *n.* | landscape painting |
| 8. 宣传画 | 宣傳畫 | xuānchuánhuà | *n.* | picture poster |
| 9. 漫画 | 漫畫 | mànhuà | *n.* | caricature; cartoon |
| 10. 铅笔画 | 鉛筆畫 | qiānbǐhuà | *n.* | pencil drawing |
| 11. 西洋画 | 西洋畫 | xīyánghuà | *n.* | Western painting |
| 12. 油画 | 油畫 | yóuhuà | *n.* | oil painting |

## 一、连接四字词组
*Match the idioms and phrases*

.................................................................................

1. 特殊           到老

2. 健康           意思

3. 荣华           长寿

4. 双喜           延年

5. 白头           富贵

6. 松鹤           临门

## 二、选择合适的词语完成句子
*Choose the most appropriate phrase to complete the sentence*

.................................................................................

1. 中国人喜欢中国画儿，是因为
     a. 中国画儿非常好看但是没有意思。
     b. 中国画儿有很多很多特殊的意思。
     c. 中国画儿又好看又有特殊的意思。

# 練習

## Exercises

## 一、連接四字詞組
*Match the idioms and phrases*

1. 特殊　　　　到老
2. 健康　　　　意思
3. 榮華　　　　長壽
4. 雙喜　　　　延年
5. 白頭　　　　富貴
6. 松鶴　　　　臨門

## 二、選擇合適的詞語完成句子
*Choose the most appropriate phrase to complete the sentence*

1. 中國人喜歡中國畫兒，是因為
   a. 中國畫兒非常好看但是沒有意思。
   b. 中國畫兒有很多很多特殊的意思。
   c. 中國畫兒又好看又有特殊的意思。

2. 中国画儿上的牡丹花代表
    a. 大福大贵。
    b. 健康长寿。
    c. 夫妻相爱。

3. 中国人喜欢喜鹊，是因为
    a. 一对喜鹊到老都不分离。
    b. 喜鹊表示你的喜事到来。
    c. 喜鹊表示可以健康长寿。

4. 中国画儿上的松树和仙鹤表示
    a. 健康长寿。
    b. 双喜临门。
    c. 白头到老。

三、找出正确答案
*Choose the correct answer*

1. "鸳鸯游水"的画儿有什么特殊的意思?
    a. 表示多生孩子。
    b. 表示白头到老。
    c. 表示双喜临门。

2. 画有两只喜鹊的画儿有什么特殊的含义?
    a. 表示双喜临门。
    b. 表示多生孩子。
    c. 表示健康长寿。

2. 中國畫兒上的牡丹花代表
   - a. 大福大貴。
   - b. 健康長壽。
   - c. 夫妻相愛。

3. 中國人喜歡喜鵲，是因為
   - a. 一對喜鵲到老都不分離。
   - b. 喜鵲表示你的喜事到來。
   - c. 喜鵲表示可以健康長壽。

4. 中國畫兒上的松樹和仙鶴表示
   - a. 健康長壽。
   - b. 雙喜臨門。
   - c. 白頭到老。

## 三、找出正確答案
*Choose the correct answer*

1. "鴛鴦游水"的畫兒有什麼特殊的意思?
   - a. 表示多生孩子。
   - b. 表示白頭到老。
   - c. 表示雙喜臨門。

2. 畫有兩隻喜鵲的畫兒有什麼特殊的含義?
   - a. 表示雙喜臨門。
   - b. 表示多生孩子。
   - c. 表示健康長壽。

3. 中国人希望新婚夫妇白头到老，送什么画儿？
    a. 送松树仙鹤画儿。
    b. 送鸳鸯游水画儿。
    c. 送有蝙蝠的画儿。

4. 蝙蝠跟什么有关系？
    a. 跟健康长寿有关。
    b. 跟喜事的喜有关。
    c. 跟福气的福有关。

## 四、思考问题，说说你的看法

*Think about the questions and talk about your perspective*

1. 中国人是怎样用画儿来表示人们的希望的？

2. 你们国家是用哪些方法表示人们的希望的？

3. 中国人喜欢中国画儿跟外国人喜欢中国画儿有什么不同？

4. 你认为中国画儿和西方画儿最大的不同是什么？

3. 中國人希望新婚夫婦白頭到老，送什麼畫兒？
　　a. 送松樹仙鶴畫兒。
　　b. 送鴛鴦游水畫兒。
　　c. 送有蝙蝠的畫兒。

4. 蝙蝠跟什麼有關系？
　　a. 跟健康長壽有關。
　　b. 跟喜事的喜有關。
　　c. 跟福氣的福有關。

四、思考問題，說說你的看法
*Think about the questions and talk about your perspective*

1. 中國人是怎樣用畫兒來表示人們的希望的？

2. 你們國家是用哪些方法表示人們的希望的？

3. 中國人喜歡中國畫兒跟外國人喜歡中國畫兒有什麼
　 不同？

4. 你認為中國畫兒和西方畫兒最大的不同是什麼？

# 七

◆ 太阳的远近 ◆
◆ 太陽的遠近 ◆

## How Far Away Is The Sun?

孔子是中国历史上有名的思想家、教育家。孔子很有学问，很多事情他都知道，所以大家都非常尊敬他，把他叫做圣人。

一天，孔子坐车去旅行，在路上他看到路边儿有两个小孩子大声地争论着什么，于是就下车走过去问小孩子："小朋友，你们在争论什么呢？"

两个小孩子看到孔子来了都非常高兴，就一起问孔子说："先生，您说太阳早上离我们近，还是中午离我们近？"

一个小孩子还没有等孔子回答，就抢着说："当然是早上离我们近了。您看，早上的太阳就和您车上的伞盖一样大，可是中午的太阳却只有小盘子那么大。这不就是远的东西显得小，近的东西显得大的道理吗？"

孔子刚要点头说对，另一个小孩子赶紧说："不对，不对！先生您想想，早晨太阳刚出来的时候，天气很凉，可是到了中午的时候，天气就很热了。这不就是离热的东西近就觉得热，离热的东西远就觉得凉的道理吗？"

孔子觉得这个小孩子说的也对。他想了一会儿，认为两个小孩子说的都有道理。这个时候孔子也胡涂了，他也弄不清楚太阳到底是早上近，还是中午近。

两个小孩子看到孔子连这么简单的事情都不知道，就一起笑了起来，说："哎呀！谁说您什么都知道啊？您原来跟我们一样啊！"

孔子是中國歷史上有名的思想家、教育家。孔子很有學問，很多事情他都知道，所以大家都非常尊敬他，把他叫做聖人。

一天，孔子坐車去旅行，在路上他看到路邊兒有兩個小孩子大聲地爭論著什麼，於是就下車走過去問小孩子：「小朋友，你們在爭論什麼呢？」

兩個小孩子看到孔子來了都非常高興，就一起問孔子說：「先生，您說太陽早上離我們近，還是中午離我們近？」

一個小孩子還沒有等孔子回答，就搶著說：「當然是早上離我們近了。您看，早上的太陽就和您車上的傘蓋一樣大，可是中午的太陽卻只有小盤子那麼大。這不就是遠的東西顯得小，近的東西顯得大的道理嗎？」

孔子剛要點頭說對，另一個小孩子趕緊說：「不對，不對！先生您想想，早晨太陽剛出來的時候，天氣很涼，可是到了中午的時候，天氣就很熱了。這不就是離熱的東西近就覺得熱，離熱的東西遠就覺得涼的道理嗎？」

孔子覺得這個小孩子說的也對。他想了一會兒，認為兩個小孩子說的都有道理。這個時候孔子也糊塗了，他也弄不清楚太陽到底是早上近，還是中午近。

兩個小孩子看到孔子連這麼簡單的事情都不知道，就一起笑了起來，說：「哎呀！誰說您什麼都知道啊？您原來跟我們一樣啊！」

| Simplified Characters | Traditional Characters | Pinyin | Part of Speech | English Definition |
|---|---|---|---|---|
| 1. 远近 | 遠近 | yuǎnjìn | *n.* | distance |
| 2. 历史 | 歷史 | lìshǐ | *n.* | history |
| 3. 有名 | 有名 | yǒumíng | *adj.* | well-known; famous |
| 4. 学问 | 學問 | xuéwen | *n.* | knowledge |
| 5. 尊敬 | 尊敬 | zūnjìng | *v.* | respect |
| 6. 思想家 | 思想家 | sīxiǎngjiā | *n.* | ideologist; thinker |
| 7. 教育家 | 教育家 | jiàoyùjiā | *n.* | educator |
| 8. 圣人 | 聖人 | shèngrén | *n.* | sage; wise person |
| 9. 旅行 | 旅行 | lǚxíng | *v.* | travel |
| 10. 争论 | 爭論 | zhēnglùn | *v.* | argue; debate |
| 11. 离 | 離 | lí | *v.* | away; from |
| 12. 抢着 | 搶著 | qiǎngzhe | *v.* | scramble for; fight over |
| 13. 当然 | 當然 | dāngrán | *adv.* | of course |
| 14. 伞盖 | 傘蓋 | sǎngài | *n.* | umbrella cover (over a cart) |
| 15. 却 | 卻 | què | *conj.* | but |

| Simplified Characters | Traditional Characters | Pinyin | Part of Speech | English Definition |
|---|---|---|---|---|
| 16. 盘子 | 盤子 | pánzi | *n.* | plate |
| 17. 显得 | 顯得 | xiǎnde | *v.* | look like; appear to be |
| 18. 道理 | 道理 | dàoli | *n.* | principle; truth |
| 19. 点头 | 點頭 | diǎn tóu | *vo.* | nod one's head |
| 20. 赶紧 | 趕緊 | gǎnjǐn | *adv.* | immediately |
| 21. 早晨 | 早晨 | zǎochén | *n.* | (early) morning |
| 22. 凉 | 涼 | liáng | *adj.* | cold |
| 23. 到底 | 到底 | dàodǐ | *adv.* | after all; in the end |
| 24. 胡涂 | 糊塗 | hútu | *adj.* | confusing; muddled |
| 25. 弄 | 弄 | nòng | *v.* | make; do |
| 26. 清楚 | 清楚 | qīngchǔ | *adj.* | clearly understood; distinct |
| 27. 这么 | 這麼 | zhème | *pn.* | so; such |
| 28. 简单 | 簡單 | jiǎndān | *adj.* | simple |
| 29. 哎呀 | 哎呀 | āi yā | *interj.* | Ah! |
| 30. 原来 | 原來 | yuánlái | *adv.* | originally |

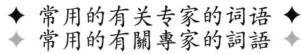

◆ 常用的有关专家的词语 ◆
◆ 常用的有關專家的詞語 ◆

Commonly Used Related Words and Phrase

| | Simplified Characters | Traditional Characters | Pinyin | Part of Speech | English Definition |
|---|---|---|---|---|---|
| 1. | 专家 | 專家 | zhuānjiā | n. | expert; specialist |
| 2. | 科学家 | 科學家 | kēxuéjiā | n. | scientist |
| 3. | 政治家 | 政治家 | zhèngzhìjiā | n. | statesman; politician |
| 4. | 哲学家 | 哲學家 | zhéxuéjiā | n. | philosopher |
| 5. | 艺术家 | 藝術家 | yìshùjiā | n. | artist |
| 6. | 音乐家 | 音樂家 | yīnyuèjiā | n. | musician |
| 7. | 数学家 | 數學家 | shùxuéjiā | n. | mathematician |
| 8. | 化学家 | 化學家 | huàxuéjiā | n. | chemist |
| 9. | 物理学家 | 物理學家 | wùlǐxuéjiā | n. | physicist |
| 10. | 经济学家 | 經濟學家 | jīngjìxuéjiā | n. | economist |

故事出處：《列子·湯問》

　　原文：孔子東游，見兩小兒辯鬥，問其故。一兒曰：「我以日始出時去人近，而日中時遠也。」一兒以日初出遠，而日中時近也。一兒曰：「日初出大如車蓋，及日中，則如盤盂，此不為遠者小而近者大乎？」一兒曰：「日初出滄滄涼涼，及其日中如探湯，此不為近者熱而遠者涼乎？」孔子不能決也。兩小兒笑曰：「孰為汝多知乎？」

# 练习

## Exercises

一、 连接意思相近的词语

*Link the similar words*

| 1. 学问 | 明白 |
|---|---|
| 2. 认为 | 气候 |
| 3. 争论 | 觉得 |
| 4. 清楚 | 早晨 |
| 5. 天气 | 知识 |
| 6. 早上 | 辩论 |

二、 选择合适的词语完成句子

*Choose the most appropriatephrase to complete the sentence*

1. 大家把孔子叫做圣人，是因为
    a. 他年纪很大。
    b. 他喜欢旅行。
    c. 他很有学问。

## 一、連接意思相近的詞語

*Link the similar words*

1. 學問　　　　　明白

2. 認為　　　　　氣候

3. 爭論　　　　　覺得

4. 清楚　　　　　早晨

5. 天氣　　　　　知識

6. 早上　　　　　辯論

## 二、選擇合適的詞語完成句子

*Choose the most appropriate phrase to complete the sentence*

1. 大家把孔子叫做聖人，是因為
   a. 他年紀很大。
   b. 他喜歡旅行。
   c. 他很有學問。

2. 两个小孩子看到孔子来了很高兴，是因为
    a. 孔子来和他们说话。
    b. 孔子知道很多事情。
    c. 孔子的车子很漂亮。

3. 两个小孩子在争论
    a. 早上太阳大还是中午太阳大。
    b. 早上太阳热还是中午太阳热。
    c. 早上太阳近还是中午太阳近。

4. 孔子觉得
    a. 两个小孩子说得都对。
    b. 第一个小孩子说得对。
    c. 第二个小孩子说得对。

三、找出正确答案

*Choose the correct answer*

1. 孔子为什么要下车问小孩子问题？
    a. 因为他非常喜欢跟小孩子谈话。
    b. 因为他想知道小孩子争论什么。
    c. 因为他坐车旅行看路边的小孩子。

2. 孔子为什么没有办法回答小孩子的问题？
    a. 因为他不想让两个小孩子不高兴。
    b. 因为他觉得两个小孩子都有道理。
    c. 因为他觉得两个小孩子都没道理。

2. 兩個小孩子看到孔子來了很高興，是因為
    a. 孔子來和他們說話。
    b. 孔子知道很多事情。
    c. 孔子的車子很漂亮。

3. 兩個小孩子在爭論
    a. 早上太陽大還是中午太陽大。
    b. 早上太陽熱還是中午太陽熱。
    c. 早上太陽近還是中午太陽近。

4. 孔子覺得
    a. 兩個小孩子說得都對。
    b. 第一個小孩子說得對。
    c. 第二個小孩子說得對。

三、找出正確答案

*Choose the correct answer*

......................................................................

1. 孔子為什麼要下車問小孩子問題？
    a. 因為他非常喜歡跟小孩子談話。
    b. 因為他想知道小孩子爭論什麼。
    c. 因為他坐車旅行看路邊的小孩子。

2. 孔子為什麼沒有辦法回答小孩子的問題？
    a. 因為他不想讓兩個小孩子不高興。
    b. 因為他覺得兩個小孩子都有道理。
    c. 因為他覺得兩個小孩子都沒道理。

3. 两个小孩子为什么笑孔子？
    a. 因为孔子是一个有名的教育家。
    b. 因为孔子很聪明什么事情都懂。
    c. 因为孔子不能回答他们的问题。

4. 第二个小孩子为什么认为早上太阳远？
    a. 因为早上天气凉。
    b. 因为早上太阳大。
    c. 因为早上太阳热。

四、思考问题，说说你的看法

*Think about the questions and talk about your perspective*

1. 你认为太阳早上离我们近？还是中午离我们近？

2. 近的东西显得大，远的东西显得小有没有道理？
   为什么？

3. 有学问的人是不是什么事情都知道？为什么？

4. 人们尊敬不尊敬有学问的人？为什么？

3. 兩個小孩子為什麼笑孔子?
    a. 因為孔子是一個有名的教育家。
    b. 因為孔子很聰明什麼事情都懂。
    c. 因為孔子不能回答他們的問題。

4. 第二個小孩子為什麼認為早上太陽遠?
    a. 因為早上天气涼。
    b. 因為早上太陽大。
    c. 因為早上太陽熱。

四、思考問題，說說你的看法
*Think about the questions and talk about your perspective*

1. 你認為太陽早上離我們近? 還是中午離我們近?

2. 近的東西顯得大，遠的東西顯得小有沒有道理? 為什麼?

3. 有學問的人是不是什麼事情都知道? 為什麼?

4. 人們尊敬不尊敬有學問的人? 為什麼?

# 八

◆ 自以为聪明的人 ◆
◆ 自以為聰明的人 ◆

**People Who Think They're Smart**

世上有许多聪明人，也有许多自以为聪明的人。聪明人做事情的时候，会想出一些办法来，把事情做得又快又好；自以为聪明的人做事情的时候，也会想一些办法，但是他们想出来的办法，常常把事情办坏。下面讲的就是一个自以为聪明的人做笨事情的故事。

很久以前有个人叫李明，有一年他帮朋友照看庄稼。李明天天去田里看小秧苗长高了没有，每次去的时候他都觉得小秧苗长得太慢了，好像总是那么一点点儿高，李明有些着急了。

李明要想办法让小秧苗长得快一点儿，长得高一些。这天晚上他躺在床上翻来覆去地想啊、想啊……，天快亮的时候，他终于想出来了一个好办法：把小秧苗拔高一点儿。

想到这个办法以后，李明非常兴奋，他觉得自己很聪明，很了不起。他自言自语地说："小秧苗长得慢，我们可以帮助它长快一点儿啊！大家怎么这么笨呢？怎么连这么简单的办法都想不到呢？"

李明兴奋得睡不着觉了。天刚刚亮，他就跑到田里去，一个人弯着腰把小秧苗一棵一棵地往高拔。他拔啊、拔啊……，从早上一直拔到天黑。当田里剩下最后几棵秧苗的时候，李明累得实在拔不动了，他直起腰来，摇摇晃晃地回家去了。

第二天一大早，李明就来到田里看他的秧苗。他发现昨天辛辛苦苦拔高的秧苗全都死了，只有那几棵没有拔的小秧苗直直地站立着，这时候他突然觉得这几棵秧苗一夜之间好像长高了许多。

世上有許多聰明人，也有許多自以為聰明的人。聰明人做事情的時候，會想出一些辦法來，把事情做得又快又好；自以為聰明的人做事情的時候，也會想一些辦法，但是他們想出來的辦法，常常把事情辦壞。下面講的就是一個自以為聰明的人做笨事情的故事。

很久以前有個人叫李明，有一年他幫朋友照看莊稼。李明天天去田裡看小秧苗長高了沒有，每次去的時候他都覺得小秧苗長得太慢了，好像總是那麼一點點兒高，李明有些著急了。

李明要想辦法讓小秧苗長得快一點兒，長得高一些。這天晚上他躺在床上翻來覆去地想啊、想啊……，天快亮的時候，他終於想出來了一個好辦法：把小秧苗拔高一點兒。

想到這個辦法以後，李明非常興奮，他覺得自己很聰明，很了不起。他自言自語地說：「小秧苗長得慢，我們可以幫助它長快一點兒啊！大家怎麼這麼笨呢？怎麼連這麼簡單的辦法都想不到呢？」

李明興奮得睡不著覺了。天剛剛亮，他就跑到田裡去，一個人彎著腰把小秧苗一棵一棵地往高拔。他拔啊、拔啊……，從早上一直拔到天黑。當田裡剩下最後幾棵秧苗的時候，李明累得實在拔不動了，他直起腰來，搖搖晃晃地回家去了。

第二天一大早，李明就來到田裡看他的秧苗。他發現昨天辛辛苦苦拔高的秧苗全都死了，只有那幾棵沒有拔的小秧苗直直地站立著，這時候他突然覺得這幾棵秧苗一夜之間好像長高了許多。

| Simplified Characters | Traditional Characters | Pinyin | Part of Speech | English Definition |
|---|---|---|---|---|
| 1. 世上 | 世上 | shìshang | *n.* | world |
| 2. 自以为 | 自以為 | zìyǐwéi | *v.* | believe oneself to be… |
| 3. 办 | 辦 | bàn | *v.* | do |
| 4. 笨 | 笨 | bèn | *adj.* | stupid; foolish |
| 5. 照看 | 照看 | zhàokàn | *v.* | look after; keep an eye on |
| 6. 庄稼 | 莊稼 | zhuāngjia | *n.* | crops |
| 7. 田 | 田 | tián | *n.* | field |
| 8. 秧苗 | 秧苗 | yāngmiáo | *n.* | rice seedling |
| 9. 长 | 長 | zhǎng | *v.* | grow |
| 10. 总是 | 總是 | zǒngshì | *adv.* | always |
| 11. 一点点儿 | 一點點兒 | yīdiǎndiǎnr | *adj.* | a little |
| 12. 躺 | 躺 | tǎng | *v.* | lay down; recline |
| 13. 翻来复去 | 翻來復去 | fānláifùqù | *id.* | toss and turn |
| 14. 天亮 | 天亮 | tiānliàng | *n.* | daybreak; dawn; daylight |

| | Simplified Characters | Traditional Characters | Pinyin | Part of Speech | English Definition |
|---|---|---|---|---|---|
| 15. | 终于 | 終於 | zhōngyú | *adv.* | finally |
| 16. | 拔 | 拔 | bá | *v.* | pull up |
| 17. | 兴奋 | 興奮 | xīngfèn | *adj.* | be excited |
| 18. | 了不起 | 了不起 | liǎobuqǐ | *adj.* | extraordinary; unbelievable |
| 19. | 自言自语 | 自言自語 | zìyánzìyǔ | *id.* | talk to oneself |
| 20. | 往 | 往 | wǎng | *prep.* | toward |
| 21. | 弯腰 | 彎腰 | wānyāo | *vo.* | bend one's waist; stoop |
| 22. | 剩下 | 剩下 | shèngxià | *v.* | be left (over); remain |
| 23. | 实在 | 實在 | shízài | *adv.* | really; in reality |
| 24. | 直起腰 | 直起腰 | zhíqǐyāo | *v.* | straighten one's back |
| 25. | 摇摇晃晃 | 搖搖晃晃 | yáoyáo-huànghuàng | *adj.* | tottering; shaky |
| 26. | 发现 | 發現 | fāxiàn | *v.* | find; discover |
| 27. | 辛辛苦苦 | 辛辛苦苦 | xīnxīnkǔkǔ | *adj.* | laboriously; strenuously |
| 28. | 直直 | 直直 | zhízhí | *adj.* | straight; upright; vertical |
| 29. | 站立 | 站立 | zhànlì | *v.* | stand erect; stand upright |
| 30. | 之间 | 之間 | zhījiān | *n.* | between; among; while |

# ✦ 常用的有关粮食的词语 ✦
# ✦ 常用的有關糧食的詞語 ✦

## Commonly Used Related Words and Phrases

| | Simplified Characters | Traditional Characters | Pinyin | Part of Speech | English Definition |
|---|---|---|---|---|---|
| 1. | 粮食 | 糧食 | liángshi | *n.* | grain; cereals |
| 2. | 麦子 | 麥子 | màizi | *n.* | wheat |
| 3. | 燕麦 | 燕麥 | yànmài | *n.* | oats |
| 4. | 面粉 | 麵粉 | miànfěn | *n.* | wheat flour; flour |
| 5. | 稻子 | 稻子 | dàozi | *n.* | rice; paddy |
| 6. | 大米 | 大米 | dàmǐ | *n.* | (husked) rice |
| 7. | 小米 | 小米 | xiǎomǐ | *n.* | millet |
| 8. | 玉米 | 玉米 | yùmǐ | *n.* | corn |
| 9. | 红薯 | 紅薯 | hóngshǔ | *n.* | yam |
| 10. | 土豆 | 土豆 | tǔdòu | *n.* | potato |
| 11. | 豆子 | 豆子 | dòuzi | *n.* | beans or peas |

故事出處：《孟子·公孫丑上》

原文：宋人有憫其苗之不長而揠之者，芒芒然歸，謂其人曰："今日病矣！予助苗長矣。"其子趨而往視之，苗則槁矣。

---

# 练习

## Exercises

---

## 一、连接意思相反的词语
*Link the antonyms*

........................................................................................................

1. 聪明             天亮

2. 高                  复杂

3. 躺                  许多

4. 简单             笨

5. 天黑             低

6. 一点儿         站

## 二、选择合适的词语完成句子
*Choose the most appropriate phrase to complete the sentence*

........................................................................................................

1. 自以为聪明的人
    a. 常常想不出办法来。
    b. 常常会做出大事情。
    c. 常常会把事情办坏。

## 一、連接意思相反的詞語

*Link the antonyms*

1. 聰明            天亮

2. 高                複雜

3. 躺                許多

4. 簡單            笨

5. 天黑            低

6. 一點兒         站

## 二、選擇合適的詞語完成句子

*Choose the most appropriate phrase to complete the sentence*

1. 自以為聰明的人
   a. 常常想不出辦法來。
   b. 常常會做出大事情。
   c. 常常會把事情辦坏。

2. 李明觉得自己很聪明，是因为
    a. 他能把小秧苗都拔高。
    b. 他能想出很好的办法。
    c. 他能躺在床上想办法。

3. 李明有些着急，是因为
    a. 田里的小秧苗长得太慢了。
    b. 田里的小秧苗长得太快了。
    c. 田里的小秧苗长得太多了。

4. 李明晚上翻来复去不睡觉，是因为
    a. 他看到秧苗长得很高，很高兴。
    b. 他想办法让秧苗长高，很着急。
    c. 他把秧苗都拔高了许多，很累。

## 三、找出正确答案
*Choose the correct answer*

1. 为什么李明要把小秧苗拔高？
    a. 每天没有事情做。
    b. 觉得自己很聪明。
    c. 要帮助秧苗长高。

2. 李明是怎么拔苗的？
    a. 一个人弯腰拔小秧苗。
    b. 翻来复去地拔小秧苗。
    c. 摇摇晃晃地拔小秧苗。

2. 李明覺得自己很聰明，是因為
    a. 他能把小秧苗都拔高。
    b. 他能想出很好的辦法。
    c. 他能躺在床上想辦法。

3. 李明有些著急，是因為
    a. 田裡的小秧苗長得太慢了。
    b. 田裡的小秧苗長得太快了。
    c. 田裡的小秧苗長得太多了。

4. 李明晚上翻來復去不睡覺，是因為
    a. 他看到秧苗長得很高，很高興。
    b. 他想辦法讓秧苗長高，很著急。
    c. 他把秧苗都拔高了許多，很累。

## 三、找出正確答案
*Choose the correct answer*

1. 為什麼李明要把小秧苗拔高？
    a. 每天沒有事情做。
    b. 覺得自己很聰明。
    c. 要幫助秧苗長高。

2. 李明是怎麼拔苗的？
    a. 一個人彎腰拔小秧苗。
    b. 翻來覆去地拔小秧苗。
    c. 搖搖晃晃地拔小秧苗。

3. 为什么田里剩下最后几棵秧苗?
    a. 李明要看看拔过的秧苗和没拔过的有什么不同。
    b. 李明从早上一直拔到天黑他累得实在拔不动了。
    c. 李明想让大家看看他拔过的秧苗比没拔过的高。

4. 第二天一大早李明到田里发现了什么?
    a. 一夜之间秧苗长高了许多。
    b. 秧苗总是那么一点点儿高。
    c. 被他拔过的秧苗全都死了。

## 四、思考问题，说说你的看法
*Think about the questions and talk about your perspective*

1. 自以为聪明有什么不好? 为什么?

2. 怎么才可以不做自以为聪明的人?

3. 为什么他觉得没有拔过的秧苗好像长高了许多?

4. 聪明人和自以为聪明的人有什么不同?

3. 為什麼田裡剩下最後幾棵秧苗?
　　a. 李明要看看拔過的秧苗和沒拔過的有什麼不同。
　　b. 李明從早上一直拔到天黑他累得實在拔不動了。
　　c. 李明想讓大家看看他拔過的秧苗比沒拔過的高。

4. 第二天一大早李明到田裡發現了什麼?
　　a. 一夜之間秧苗長高了許多。
　　b. 秧苗總是那麼一點點兒高。
　　c. 被他拔過的秧苗全都死了。


四、思考問題，說說你的看法
*Think about the questions and talk about your perspective*

1. 自以為聰明有什麼不好? 為什麼?

2. 怎麼才可以不做自以為聰明的人?

3. 為什麼他覺得沒有拔過的秧苗好像長高了許多?

4. 聰明人和自以為聰明的人有什麼不同?

# 九

◆ 有礼貌地称呼人 ◆
◆ 有禮貌地稱呼人 ◆

Addressing People Politely

中国人在称呼上特别讲究礼貌。他们在问别人姓什么的时候，会很有礼貌地说："您贵姓？"如果问的是一位年纪很大的人，他们还会更有礼貌地说："老人家，您老贵姓？"

中国人喜欢用家庭成员的称谓来称呼那些年纪大的人，比如说，见到跟父母年纪差不多大的人，就要叫人家叔叔、阿姨、伯伯、伯母；要是见到年纪更大的人，就叫人家爷爷、奶奶。用家庭成员的称谓来称呼年纪大的人，也是一种礼貌的做法。

父母教育孩子要尊敬大人。他们告诉孩子叫人的时候要注意年龄，千万别叫错了。如果遇到一个人，你弄不清楚应该叫他哥哥，还是叫他叔叔，那么就叫他叔叔；弄不清楚应该叫他叔叔，还是叫他爷爷，那么就叫他爷爷。总之，要往高叫，往高叫也表示一种礼貌。

父母们还特别告诉孩子，一定不能叫年纪大的人的名字。中国人认为，叫年纪大的人的名字是最不礼貌的做法。当然，对于坏人，即使是年纪大的人，也不能叫他们叔叔、阿姨、爷爷、奶奶什么的。

西方国家的称呼习惯跟中国不完全一样，西方国家的小孩子有时候可以直接叫大人的名字。在西方国家的中小学里，学生和大人一样都把老师叫做"先生、女士"或者"小姐"什么的。

在中国的学校里，特别是中小学里，学生一定得很尊敬地把老师叫做"老师"。如果一个学生随随便便地把老师叫"先生、女士、小姐"的话，他恐怕就得不到好成绩了。

中國人在稱呼上特別講究禮貌。他們在問別人姓什麼的時候，會很有禮貌地說："您貴姓？"如果問的是一位年紀很大的人，他們還會更有禮貌地說："老人家，您老貴姓？"

中國人喜歡用家庭成員的稱謂來稱呼那些年紀大的人，比如說，見到跟父母年紀差不多大的人，就要叫人家叔叔、阿姨、伯伯、伯母；要是見到年紀更大的人，就叫人家爺爺、奶奶。用家庭成員的稱謂來稱呼年紀大的人，也是一種禮貌的做法。

父母教育孩子要尊敬大人。他們告訴孩子叫人的時候要注意年齡，千萬別叫錯了。如果遇到一個人，你弄不清楚應該叫他哥哥，還是叫他叔叔，那麼就叫他叔叔；弄不清楚應該叫他叔叔，還是叫他爺爺，那麼就叫他爺爺。總之，要往高叫，往高叫也表示一種禮貌。

父母們還特別告訴孩子，一定不能叫年紀大的人的名字。中國人認為，叫年紀大的人的名字是最不禮貌的做法。當然，對於壞人，即使是年紀大的人，也不能叫他們叔叔、阿姨、爺爺、奶奶什麼的。

西方國家的稱呼習慣跟中國不完全一樣，西方國家的小孩子有時候可以直接叫大人的名字。在西方國家的中小學裡，學生和大人一樣都把老師叫做"先生、女士"或者"小姐"什麼的。

在中國的學校裡，特別是中小學裡，學生一定得很尊敬地把老師叫做"老師"。如果一個學生隨隨便便地把老師叫"先生、女士、小姐"的話，他恐怕就得不到好成績了。

New Vocabulary

| | Simplified Characters | Traditional Characters | Pinyin | Part of Speech | English Definition |
|---|---|---|---|---|---|
| 1. | 礼貌 | 禮貌 | lǐmào | n. | courtesy; manners |
| 2. | 称呼 | 稱呼 | chēnghu | n. | form of address |
| 3. | 讲究 | 講究 | jiǎngjiu | v. | pay attention to; stress |
| 4. | 年纪 (龄) | 年紀 (齡) | niánjì (líng) | n. | age |
| 5. | 老人家 | 老人家 | lǎorénjia | n. | a polite form of address to an elderly person |
| 6. | 您老 | 您老 | nínlǎo | n. | a polite form of address to an elderly person |
| 7. | 家庭 | 家庭 | jiātíng | n. | family |
| 8. | 成员 | 成員 | chéngyuán | n. | member |
| 9. | 称谓 | 稱謂 | chēngwèi | n. | appellation; title |
| 10. | 做法 | 做法 | zuòfa | n. | way of doing things |
| 11. | 人家 | 人家 | rénjia | n. | other people |
| 12. | 教育 | 教育 | jiàoyù | v. | educate |

| | Simplified Characters | Traditional Characters | Pinyin | Part of Speech | English Definition |
|---|---|---|---|---|---|
| 13. | 叫人 | 叫人 | jiàorén | *vo.* | address somebody respectfully |
| 14. | 注意 | 注意 | zhùyì | *v.* | pay attention to |
| 15. | 千万 | 千萬 | qiānwàn | *adv.* | must; make sure to |
| 16. | 弄不清楚 | 弄不清楚 | nòngbū qīngchǔ | *vc.* | can't get it clear |
| 17. | 应该 | 應該 | yīnggāi | *v.* | should; ought to |
| 18. | 总之 | 總之 | zǒngzhī | *conj.* | in a word; in short |
| 19. | 表示 | 表示 | biǎoshì | *v.* | express; indicate |
| 20. | 对于 | 對於 | duìyú | *prep.* | for |
| 21. | 即使…也 | 即使…也 | jíshǐ...yě | *conj.* | even if |
| 22. | 阿姨 | 阿姨 | āyí | *n.* | mother's sister; aunt |
| 23. | 西方 | 西方 | xīfāng | *n.* | Western |
| 24. | 习惯 | 習慣 | xíguàn | *n.* | be accustomed to; be used to |
| 25. | 完全 | 完全 | wánquán | *adj.* | complete; completely |
| 26. | 直接 | 直接 | zhíjiē | *adv.* | directly |
| 27. | 女士 | 女士 | nǔshì | *n.* | lady; madam |
| 28. | 随随便便 | 隨隨便便 | suísuí biànbiàn | *adj.* | casually |
| 29. | 恐怕 | 恐怕 | kǒngpà | *adv.* | (I'm) afraid (that); perhaps |
| 30. | 成绩 | 成績 | chéngjì | *n.* | grade; achievement |

# ◆ 常用的有关称呼的词语 ◆
# ◆ 常用的有關稱呼的詞語 ◆

## Commonly Used Related Words and Phrases

| | Simplified Characters | Traditional Characters | Pinyin | Part of Speech | English Definition |
|---|---|---|---|---|---|
| 1. | 老爷爷 | 老爺爺 | lǎoyéye | *n.* | a polite form of address to an elderly man |
| 2. | 老奶奶 | 老奶奶 | lǎonǎinai | *n.* | a polite form of address to an elderly woman |
| 3. | 老大爷 | 老大爺 | lǎodàye | *n.* | a polite form of address to an elderly man |
| 4. | 老大娘 | 老大娘 | lǎodàniáng | *n.* | a polite form of address to an elderly woman |
| 5. | 大爷 | 大爺 | dàye | *n.* | a polite form of address to an elderly man |
| 6. | 大娘 | 大娘 | dàniáng | *n.* | a polite form of address to an elderly woman |
| 7. | 大伯 | 大伯 | dàbó | *n.* | a polite form of address to an elderly man |
| 8. | 大妈 | 大媽 | dàmā | *n.* | a polite form of address to an elderly woman |
| 9. | 大叔 | 大叔 | dàshū | *n.* | a polite form of address to an elderly man |

| | Simplified Characters | Traditional Characters | Pinyin | Part of Speech | English Definition |
|---|---|---|---|---|---|
| 10. | 大婶 | 大嬸 | dàshěn | n. | a polite form of address to an elderly woman |
| 11. | 大哥 | 大哥 | dàgē | n. | a polite form of address to a man about one's own age |
| 12. | 大姐 | 大姐 | dàjiě | n. | a polite form of address to a woman about one's own age |
| 13. | 先生 | 先生 | xiānsheng | n. | mister (Mr.); gentleman; sir |
| 14. | 小姐 | 小姐 | xiǎojie | n. | miss; young lady |
| 15. | 同志 | 同志 | tóngzhì | n. | comrade |
| 16. | 师傅 | 師傅 | shīfu | n. | master; a polite form of address to people |

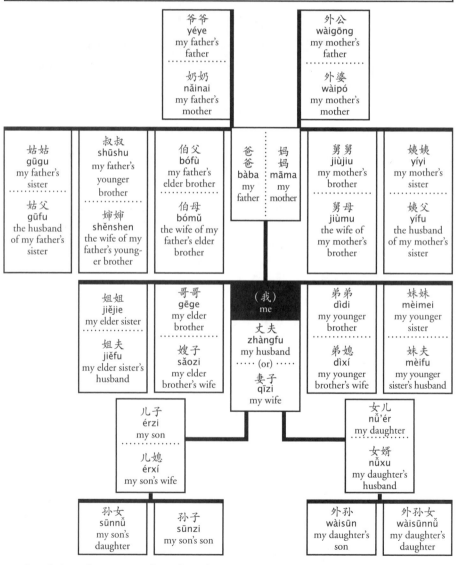

# 中国家庭称谓简表

## Chinese Family Relationships

| | |
|---|---|
| 爷爷 yéye my father's father | 外公 wàigōng my mother's father |
| 奶奶 nǎinai my father's mother | 外婆 wàipó my mother's mother |

| 姑姑 gūgu my father's sister | 叔叔 shūshu my father's younger brother | 伯父 bófù my father's elder brother | 爸爸 bàba my father | 妈妈 māma my mother | 舅舅 jiùjiu my mother's brother | 姨姨 yíyi my mother's sister |
|---|---|---|---|---|---|---|
| 姑父 gūfu the husband of my father's sister | 婶婶 shěnshen the wife of my father's younger brother | 伯母 bómǔ the wife of my father's elder brother | | | 舅母 jiùmu the wife of my mother's brother | 姨父 yífu the husband of my mother's sister |

| 姐姐 jiějie my elder sister | 哥哥 gēge my elder brother | （我） me | 弟弟 dìdi my younger brother | 妹妹 mèimei my younger sister |
|---|---|---|---|---|
| 姐夫 jiěfu my elder sister's husband | 嫂子 sǎozi my elder brother's wife | 丈夫 zhàngfu my husband ⋯⋯ (or) ⋯⋯ 妻子 qīzi my wife | 弟媳 dìxí my younger brother's wife | 妹夫 mèifu my younger sister's husband |

| 儿子 érzi my son | 女儿 nǚ'ér my daughter |
|---|---|
| 儿媳 érxí my son's wife | 女婿 nǚxu my daughter's husband |

| 孙女 sūnnǚ my son's daughter | 孙子 sūnzi my son's son | 外孙 wàisūn my daughter's son | 外孙女 wàisūnnǚ my daughter's daughter |
|---|---|---|---|

*The above information is based on the Contemporary Chinese Dictionary, 2002.*

# 中國家庭稱謂簡表

## Chinese Family Relationships

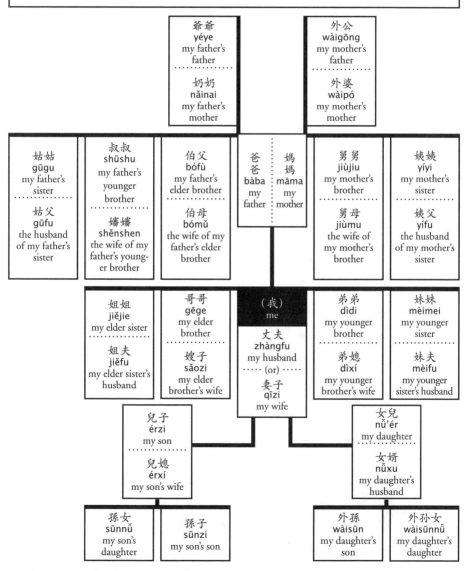

The above information is based on the Contemporary Chinese Dictionary, 2002.

| 练习 |
| :---: |
| Exercises |

一、选择合适的词语完成句子

*Choose the most appropriate phrase to complete the sentence*

1. 中国人在问年纪大的人姓什么的时候，会有礼貌地说
   a. 你叫什么。
   b. 你姓什么。
   c. 您老贵姓。

2. 中国人见到跟自己父母年纪差不多大的人，要叫人家
   a. 爷爷、奶奶。
   b. 叔叔、阿姨。
   c. 大哥、大姐。

3. 父母告诉孩子一定不可以
   a. 叫年纪大的人名字。
   b. 叫年纪大的人叔叔。
   c. 叫年纪大的人爷爷。

4. 西方国家的称呼习惯跟中国不一样，因为
   a. 小孩子不能直接叫爸爸的名字。
   b. 中小学学生不能叫老师的名字。
   c. 学生可以叫老师"先生，女士"。

一、選擇合適的詞語完成句子
*Choose the most appropriate phrase to complete the sentence*

1. 中國人在問年紀大的人姓什麼的時候，會有禮貌地說
   a. 你叫什麼。
   b. 你姓什麼。
   c. 您老貴姓。

2. 中國人見到跟自己父母年紀差不多大的人，要叫人家
   a. 爺爺、奶奶。
   b. 叔叔、阿姨。
   c. 大哥、大姐。

3. 父母告訴孩子一定不可以
   a. 叫年紀大的人名字。
   b. 叫年紀大的人叔叔。
   c. 叫年紀大的人爺爺。

4. 西方國家的稱呼習慣跟中國不一樣，因為
   a. 小孩子不能直接叫爸爸的名字。
   b. 中小學學生不能叫老師的名字。
   c. 學生可以叫老師"先生，女士"。

## 二、填写相关的词
*Fill in the blank with the appropriate choice*

1. 把跟父母年纪差不多大的人叫＿＿＿＿＿＿＿＿＿＿＿。

2. 把比父母年纪大的人叫＿＿＿＿＿＿＿＿＿＿＿。

3. 把比自己年纪大的人叫＿＿＿＿＿＿＿＿＿＿＿。

4. 把比自己年纪小的人叫＿＿＿＿＿＿＿＿＿＿＿。

爷爷、奶奶、叔叔、阿姨、大哥、大姐、外婆、外公、小弟、小妹、伯伯、伯母

## 三、找出正确答案
*Choose the correct answer*

1. 中国人在称呼上怎样讲究礼貌？
   a. 可以叫年纪大的人的名字。
   b. 可以叫老师和父母的名字。
   c. 不能叫年纪大的人的名字。

2. 遇到一个人你不知道该叫他伯伯还是爷爷，你应该怎样称呼？
   a. 叫他爷爷。
   b. 叫他叔叔。
   c. 叫他伯伯。

## 二、 填寫相關的詞
*Fill in the blank with the appropriate choice*

1. 把跟父母年紀差不多大的人叫＿＿＿＿＿＿＿＿＿。

2. 把比父母年紀大的人叫＿＿＿＿＿＿＿＿＿。

3. 把比自己年紀大的人叫＿＿＿＿＿＿＿＿＿。

4. 把比自己年紀小的人叫＿＿＿＿＿＿＿＿＿。

　　爺爺、奶奶、叔叔、阿姨、大哥、大姐、外婆、
　　外公、小弟、小妹、伯伯、伯母


## 三、 找出正確答案
*Choose the correct answer*

1. 中國人在稱呼上怎樣講究禮貌?
    a. 可以叫年紀大的人的名字。
    b. 可以叫老師和父母的名字。
    c. 不能叫年紀大的人的名字。

2. 遇到一個人你不知道該叫他伯伯還是爺爺，你應該怎樣稱呼?
    a. 叫他爺爺。
    b. 叫他叔叔。
    c. 叫他伯伯。

3. 中国人认为最不礼貌的做法是什么?
    a. 不能随便叫别人的名字。
    b. 叫老师或者父母的名字。
    c. 把年纪大的人叫老人家。

4. 为什么用家庭成员的称谓来称呼那些年纪大的人?
    a. 因为他们的名字都很难听。
    b. 因为我不知道他们的名字。
    c. 因为这是表示礼貌的做法。

四、思考问题，说说你的看法
*Think about the questions and talk about your perspective*

1. 你的国家在家庭成员称呼上有什么讲究?

2. 你认为小孩子可以直接叫大人的名字吗? 为什么?

3. 你的国家的称呼习惯和中国的称呼习惯有什么相同或者不同?

4. 如果有人用家庭成员的称谓称呼你，你会有什么感觉? 为什么?

3. 中國人認為最不禮貌的做法是什麼?
   a. 不能隨便叫別人的名字。
   b. 叫老師或者父母的名字。
   c. 把年紀大的人叫老人家。

4. 為什麼用家庭成員的稱謂來稱呼那些年紀大的人?
   a. 因為他們的名字都很難听。
   b. 因為我不知道他們的名字。
   c. 因為這是表示禮貌的做法。

四、思考問題，說說你的看法
*Think about the questions and talk about your perspective*

1. 你的國家在家庭成員稱呼上有什麼講究?

2. 你認為小孩子可以直接叫大人的名字嗎? 為什麼?

3. 你的國家的稱呼習慣和中國的稱呼習慣有什麼相同或者不同?

4. 如果有人用家庭成員的稱謂稱呼你，你會有什麼感覺? 為什麼?

# 十

♦ 独生子女长大了 ♦
♦ 獨生子女長大了 ♦

## China's Only Children Grow Up

中国现在有十三亿多人，是世界上人口最多的国家。中国政府为了控制人口增长，1979年制定了一项计划生育政策，这个政策规定每个家庭只能生一个孩子。从那以后，在中国出生的孩子大都是没有兄弟姐妹的"独生子女"。

中国人的传统思想是传宗接代，意思是要自己的子孙一代接一代地延续下去。这就是千百年来中国人想多生孩子，特别想多生男孩子的原因，这也是中国人口越来越多的原因。

现在一个家庭只能生一个孩子，这个孩子就成了家里的宝贝，爸爸、妈妈、爷爷、奶奶、外公、外婆，所有人都宠爱这个孩子。因为家里人都围着独生子女转，人们就把独生子女叫做"小太阳"；因为家里人都特别宠爱独生子女，大家也就把独生子女叫做"小皇帝"。

有人担心这些独生子女长大以后会变得比较自私，他们可能会没有朋友，会很孤独。也有人说不用担心，因为当每一个孩子都是小太阳的时候，他们谁都不是小太阳了；当每一个孩子都是小皇帝的时候，他们谁也都不是小皇帝了。

今天，中国有八千多万个独生子女，他们中许多都已经长大成人了。这些长大了的独生子女并不像人们担心的那样自私、孤独，他们有很多朋友。而且，由于很多独生子女从小受到很好的教育，所以他们在工作和生活中也显得比较能干。

当然，他们也有自己的弱点，由于他们从小被过分地宠爱，所以在遇到困难时就显得有些无能为力，而且和别人相处时常常喜欢以自己为中心。

中國現在有十三億多人，是世界上人口最多的國家。中國政府為了控制人口增長，1979年制定了一項計划生育政策，這個政策規定每個家庭只能生一個孩子。從那以後，在中國出生的孩子大都是沒有兄弟姐妹的"獨生子女"。

中國人的傳統思想是傳宗接代，意思是要自己的子孫一代接一代地延續下去。這就是千百年來中國人想多生孩子，特別想多生男孩子的原因，這也是中國人口越來越多的原因。

現在一個家庭只能生一個孩子，這個孩子就成了家裡的寶貝，爸爸、媽媽、爺爺、奶奶、外公、外婆，所有人都寵愛這個孩子。因為家裡人都圍著獨生子女轉，人們就把獨生子女叫做"小太陽"；因為家裡人都特別寵愛獨生子女，大家也就把獨生子女叫做"小皇帝"。

有人擔心這些獨生子女長大以後會變得比較自私，他們可能會沒有朋友，會很孤獨。也有人說不用擔心，因為當每一個孩子都是小太陽的時候，他們誰都不是小太陽了；當每一個孩子都是小皇帝的時候，他們誰也都不是小皇帝了。

今天，中國有八千多万個獨生子女，他們中許多都已經長大成人了。這些長大了的獨生子女并不像人們擔心的那樣自私、孤獨，他們有很多朋友。而且，由于很多獨生子女從小受到很好的教育，所以他們在工作和生活中也顯得比較能干。

當然，他們也有自己的弱點，由于他們從小被過分地寵愛，所以在遇到困難時就顯得有些無能為力，而且和別人相處時常常喜歡以自己為中心。

| Simplified Characters | Traditional Characters | Pinyin | Part of Speech | English Definition |
|---|---|---|---|---|
| 1. 独生子女 | 獨生子女 | dúshēngzǐnǚ | n. | only child |
| 2. 人口 | 人口 | rénkǒu | n. | population |
| 3. 政府 | 政府 | zhèngfǔ | n. | government |
| 4. 控制 | 控制 | kòngzhì | v. | control |
| 5. 增长 | 增長 | zēngzhǎng | v. | increase; grow |
| 6. 制定 | 制定 | zhìdìng | v. | draw up; formulate |
| 7. 项 | 項 | xiàng | m. | classifier; measure word |
| 8. 计划生育 | 計劃生育 | jìhuàshēngyù | n. | birth control |
| 9. 政策 | 政策 | zhèngcè | n. | policy |
| 10. 传统 | 傳統 | chuántǒng | n. | tradition |
| 11. 思想 | 思想 | sīxiǎng | n. | thought |
| 12. 传宗接代 | 傳宗接代 | chuánzǒng jiēdài | id. | keep the family line alive |
| 13. 代 | 代 | dài | n. | generation |
| 14. 延续 | 延續 | yánxù | v. | continue; go on |
| 15. 宝贝 | 寶貝 | bǎobèi | n. | treasure |

| | Simplified Characters | Traditional Characters | Pinyin | Part of Speech | English Definition |
|---|---|---|---|---|---|
| 16. | 宠爱 | 寵愛 | chǒngài | *v.* | pamper; dote on (somebody) |
| 17. | 围 | 圍 | wéi | *v.* | surround |
| 18. | 转 | 轉 | zhuàn | *v.* | turn around, rotate |
| 19. | 皇帝 | 皇帝 | huángdì | *n.* | emperor |
| 20. | 自私 | 自私 | zìsī | *adj.* | selfish; self-centerd |
| 21. | 孤独 | 孤獨 | gūdú | *adj.* | lonely; solitary |
| 22. | 由于 | 由於 | yóuyú | *prep.* | owing to; as a result of |
| 23. | 受到 | 受到 | shòudào | *v.* | receive |
| 24. | 能干 | 能幹 | nénggàn | *adj.* | talented; capable |
| 25. | 过分 | 過分 | guòfèn | *adj.* | excessive; over |
| 26. | 弱点 | 弱點 | ruòdiǎn | *adj.* | weakness; weak point |
| 27. | 困难 | 困難 | kùnnan | *n.* | difficulty |
| 28. | 无能为力 | 無能為力 | wúnéngwéilì | *id.* | powerless; incapable of action |
| 29. | 相处 | 相處 | xiāngchǔ | *v.* | get along (with one another) |
| 30. | 以…为… | 以…為… | yǐ…wéi… | *conj.* | consider |

| | Simplified Characters | Traditional Characters | Pinyin | Part of Speech | English Definition |
|---|---|---|---|---|---|
| 1. | 个 | 個 | gè | *m.* | unit; measure word |
| 2. | 十 | 十 | shí | *num.* | ten |
| 3. | 百 | 百 | bǎi | *num.* | hundred |
| 4. | 千 | 千 | qiān | *num.* | thousand |
| 5. | 万 | 萬 | wàn | *num.* | ten thousand |
| 6. | 十万 | 十萬 | shíwàn | *num.* | hundred thousand |
| 7. | 百万 | 百萬 | bǎiwàn | *num.* | million |
| 8. | 千万 | 千萬 | qiānwàn | *num.* | ten million |
| 9. | 亿 | 億 | yì | *num.* | hundred million |

## 一、 连接意思相反的词语

*Link the antonyms*

1. 增长        停止

2. 传统        失望

3. 子孙        减少

4. 能干        祖先

5. 希望        现代

6. 延续        无能

## 二、 选择合适的词语完成句子

*Choose the most appropriate phrase to complete the sentence*

1. 计划生育政策是为了
   a. 传宗接代。
   b. 控制人口。
   c. 生男孩子。

# 練習

## Exercises

## 一、連接意思相反的詞語
*Link the antonyms*

1. 增長　　　　　停止

2. 傳統　　　　　失望

3. 子孫　　　　　減少

4. 能干　　　　　祖輩

5. 希望　　　　　現代

6. 延續　　　　　無能

## 二、選擇合適的詞語完成句子
*Choose the most appropriate phrase to complete the sentence*

1. 計划生育政策是為了
   a. 傳宗接代。
   b. 控制人口。
   c. 生男孩子。

2. 中国人喜欢生男孩子，是因为
    a. 男孩子将来可以做皇帝。
    b. 男孩子要比女孩子聪明。
    c. 自己的家族要传宗接代。

3. 家里人都宠爱独生子女，是因为
    a. 独生子女是家里的宝贝。
    b. 独生子女是大家的皇帝。
    c. 独生子女没有兄弟姐妹。

4. 人们担心独生子女
    a. 爱吃最好吃的东西。
    b. 爱穿最漂亮的衣服。
    c. 会变得自私和孤独。

## 三、找出正确答案
*Choose the correct answer*

1. 为什么有人担心独生子女长大后比较自私？
    a. 因为家里每个人都宠爱他们。
    b. 因为他们小时候就没有朋友。
    c. 因为他们从小没有兄弟姐妹。

2. 为什么把独生子女叫做"小太阳"？
    a. 因为每个独生子女都很孤独。
    b. 因为家人都围着独生子女转。
    c. 因为每个家庭都有独生子女。

2. 中國人喜歡生男孩子，是因為
    a. 男孩子將來可以做皇帝。
    b. 男孩子要比女孩子聰明。
    c. 自己的家族要傳宗接代。

3. 家裡人都寵愛獨生子女，是因為
    a. 獨生子女是家裡的寶貝。
    b. 獨生子女是大家的皇帝。
    c. 獨生子女沒有兄弟姐妹。

4. 人們擔心獨生子女
    a. 愛吃最好吃的東西。
    b. 愛穿最漂亮的衣服。
    c. 會變得自私和孤獨。


## 三、找出正確答案

*Choose the correct answer*

1. 為什麼有人擔心獨生子女長大后比較自私？
    a. 因為家裡每個人都寵愛他們。
    b. 因為他們小時候就沒有朋友。
    c. 因為他們從小沒有兄弟姐妹。

2. 為什麼把獨生子女叫做"小太陽"？
    a. 因為每個獨生子女都很孤獨。
    b. 因為家人都圍著獨生子女轉。
    c. 因為每個家庭都有獨生子女。

3. 现在长大的独生子女怎么样?
　　a. 他们没有很多朋友。
　　b. 他们个个聪明能干。
　　c. 他们全都是小皇帝。

4. 为什么说独生子女遇到困难就显得有些无能为力?
　　a. 因为他们从小被家人过分宠爱。
　　b. 因为他们从小受到很好的教育。
　　c. 因为他们既不自私,也不孤独。

## 四、思考问题,说说你的看法
*Think about the questions and talk about your perspective*

1. 你觉得中国应该不应该制定计划生育政策? 为什么?

2. 如果你是独生子女,你会感到幸福吗? 为什么?

3. 你认为应该怎样教育独生子女?

4. 你认为中国的计划生育政策对世界人口控制有什么影响?

3. 現在長大的獨生子女怎麼樣?
    a. 他們沒有很多朋友。
    b. 他們個個聰明能干。
    c. 他們全都是小皇帝。

4. 為什麼說獨生子女遇到困難就顯得有些無能為力?
    a. 因為他們從小被家人過分寵愛。
    b. 因為他們從小受到很好的教育。
    c. 因為他們既不自私,也不孤獨。


四、思考問題, 說說你的看法

*Think about the questions and talk about your perspective*

1. 你覺得中國應該不應該制定計划生育政策? 為什麼?

2. 如果你是獨生子女, 你會感到幸福嗎? 為什麼?

3. 你認為應該怎樣教育獨生子女?

4. 你認為中國的計划生育政策對世界人口控制有什麼影
   響?

# ◆ 附录一 拼音课文 ◆

## Appendix 1 Texts with Pinyin

# 一

## 小　霞　的　网　恋
Xiǎo　Xiá　de　wǎng　liàn

---

*Xiǎo Xiá likes logging on to internet chat. She thinks*

小　霞　很　喜　欢　上　网　聊　天　儿。她　觉
Xiǎo　Xiá　hěn　xǐ　huān　shàng　wǎng　liáo　tiān　er　tā　jué

*logged on to internet chat　know a*

得　在　网　上　聊　天　儿　可　以　认　识　很
de　zài　wǎng　shang　liáo　tiān　er　kě　yǐ　rèn　shi　hěn

*lot of people, recently she logged on know*

多　人，最　近　她　在　网　上　就　认　识　了
duō　rén　zuì　jìn　tā　zài　wǎng　shang　jiù　rèn　shi　le

*one boyfriend Her parents are*

一　个　男　朋　友。小　霞　的　父　母　不　放
yī　gè　nán　péng　yǒu　Xiǎo　Xiá　de　fù　mǔ　bù　fàng

*worried she at logged on chat, scared she*

心　小　霞　在　网　上　聊　天　儿，怕　她　遇
xīn　Xiǎo　Xiá　zài　wǎng　shang　liáo　tiān　er　pà　tā　yù

*come across bad person say all day log on chat's*

到　坏　人。他　们　说　整　天　上　网　聊　天
dào　huài　rén　tā　men　shuō　zhěng　tiān　shàng　wǎng　liáo　tiān

*people certainly not good person, so*

儿　的　人　肯　定　不　是　好　人，所　以　他
er　de　rén　kěn　dìng　bù　shì　hǎo　rén　suǒ　yǐ　tā

*they Xiao Xia logged on know this*

们　对　小　霞　在　网　上　认　识　的　这　个
men　duì　Xiǎo　Xiá　zài　wǎng　shang　rèn　shi　de　zhè　gè

*boyfriend very not at rest.*

男　朋　友　很　不　放　心。
nán　péng　yǒu　hěn　bù　fàng　xīn

*Xiao Xia says to her parents: I also every day go internet*

小　霞　对　父　母　说："我　也　天　天　上　网
Xiǎo　Xiá　duì　fù　mǔ　shuō　wǒ　yě　tiān　tiān　shàng　wǎng

*I'm not a good person? Oh internet have*

啊！难　道　我　不　是　好　人　吗？网　上　有
a　nán　dào　wǒ　bù　shì　hǎo　rén　ma　wǎng　shang　yǒu

good people also have bad people. Good luck good person

好 人 也 有 坏 人。 运 气 好 的 人 遇
hǎo rén yě yǒu huài rén yùn qì hǎo de rén yù

run into good people, good fortune bad people run into bad

到 好 人, 运 气 不 好 的 人 遇 到 坏
dào hǎo rén yùn qì bù hǎo de rén yù dào huài

people. My luck is good I This

人。 我 的 运 气 好, 我 碰 见 的 这 个
rén wǒ de yùn qì hǎo wǒ pèng jiàn de zhè gè

boy friend is good person

男 朋 友 是 好 人。”
nán péng yǒu shì hǎo rén

小 霞 提 出 要 和 男 朋 友 见 面, 小
Xiǎo Xiá tí chū yào hé nán péng yǒu jiàn miàn Xiǎo

霞 的 爸 爸 不 同 意; 小 霞 说 要 请
Xiá de bà ba bù tóng yì xiǎo xiá shuō yào qǐng

男 朋 友 来 家 里, 小 霞 的 妈 妈 不
nán péng yǒu lái jiā li Xiǎo Xiá de mā ma bù

愿 意。 小 霞 觉 得 很 委 屈, 她 觉 得
yuàn yì Xiǎo Xiá jué de hěn wěi qū tā jué de

thanks wrong

爸 爸 妈 妈 一 点 儿 都 不 爱 她, 只
bà ba mā ma yī diǎn er dōu bù ài tā zhǐ

有 她 的 男 朋 友 最 爱 她。
yǒu tā de nán péng yǒu zuì ài tā

自 从 认 识 这 个 男 朋 友 以 后, 小
zì cóng rèn shi zhè gè nán péng yǒu yǐ hòu Xiǎo

霞 就 不 想 学 习 了, 她 整 天 在 网
Xiá jiù bù xiǎng xué xí le tā zhěng tiān zài wǎng

上 和 男 朋 友 聊 天 儿。 小 霞 的 父
shang hé nán péng yǒu liáo tiān er Xiǎo Xiá de fù

母 很 着 急，就 对 小 霞 说："你 把 男
mǔ hěn zháo jí jiù duì Xiǎo Xiá shuō nǐ bǎ nán

朋 友 叫 来 让 我 们 看 看。他 要 是
péng yǒu jiào lái ràng wǒ men kàn kàn tā yào shì

好 人，你 们 可 以 来 往；如 果 我 们
hǎo rén nǐ men kě yǐ lái wǎng rú guǒ wǒ men

觉 得 他 不 好，你 就 不 要 再 跟 他
jué de tā bù hǎo nǐ jiù bù yào zài gēn tā

聊 天 儿 了，好 好 学 习 吧。"
liáo tiān er le hǎo hǎo xué xí ba

小 霞 听 了 很 高 兴，马 上 给 男 朋
Xiǎo Xiá tīng le hěn gāo xìng mǎ shàng gěi nán péng

友 发 信 说："我 父 母 要 见 你，你 赶
yǒu fā xìn shuō wǒ fù mǔ yào jiàn nǐ nǐ gǎn

快 来 我 们 家 吧！"平 时 小 霞 一 写
kuài lái wǒ men jiā ba píng shí Xiǎo Xiá yī xiě

信，她 的 男 朋 友 很 快 就 回 信，可
xìn tā de nán péng yǒu hěn kuài jiù huí xìn kě

是 今 天 等 了 半 天，她 的 男 朋 友
shì jīn tiān děng le bàn tiān tā de nán péng yǒu

也 没 有 回 信。
yě méi yǒu huí xìn

小 霞 猜 想 他 的 男 朋 友 可 能 有
Xiǎo Xiá cāi xiǎng tā de nán péng yǒu kě néng yǒu

些 不 好 意 思，就 又 发 信 说："你 不
xiē bù hǎo yì si jiù yòu fā xìn shuō Nǐ bù

要 紧 张， 也 不 要 害 怕， 我 爸 爸 妈
yào jǐn zhāng yě bù yào hài pà wǒ bà ba mā

妈 都 很 和 气。" 过 了 很 长 时 间， 男
ma dōu hěn hé qì guò le hěn cháng shí jiān nán

朋 友 回 信 了， 说： "小 霞， 对 不 起， 我
péng yǒu huí xìn le shuō Xiǎo Xiá duì bu qǐ wǒ

早 就 结 婚 了。"
zǎo jiù jié hūn le

# 一

小　丽　想　跟　谁　结　婚
Xiǎo　Lì　xiǎng　gēn　shéi　jié　hūn

一 个 人 同 时 跟 两 个 人 谈 恋 爱，
yī gè rén tóng shí gēn liǎng gè rén tán liàn ài

这 叫 做 三 角 恋 爱。 三 角 恋 爱 虽
zhè jiào zuò sān jiǎo liàn ài sān jiǎo liàn ài suī

然 不 道 德， 但 是 不 违 法。 一 个 人
rán bù dào dé dàn shì bù wéi fǎ yī gè rén

同 时 和 两 个 人 结 婚， 这 叫 做 重
tóng shí hé liǎng gè rén jié hūn zhè jiào zuò chóng

婚， 重 婚 不 仅 不 道 德， 而 且 违 法。
hūn chóng hūn bù jǐn bù dào dé ér qiě wéi fǎ

同 时 跟 两 个 人 谈 恋 爱 是 不 是
tóng shí gēn liǎng gè rén tán liàn ài shì bù shì

很 幸 福 呢? 不 是。 为 什 么 呢? 因 为
hěn xìng fú ne bù shì wèi shén me ne yīn wèi

你 最 后 只 能 选 择 跟 其 中 一 个
nǐ zuì hòu zhǐ néng xuǎn zé gēn qí zhōng yī gè

人 结 婚。 在 你 爱 的 两 个 人 中 间,
rén jié hūn zài nǐ ài de liǎng gè rén zhōng jiān

选 择 跟 一 个 人 结 婚, 是 一 件 很
xuǎn zé gēn yī gè rén jié hūn shì yī jiàn hěn

痛 苦 的 事 情。 当 你 选 择 甲 的 时
tòng kǔ de shì qing dāng nǐ xuǎn zé jiǎ de shí

候，你 会 觉 得 乙 特 别 好；当 你 选
hou nǐ huì jué de yǐ tè bié hǎo dāng nǐ xuǎn

择 乙 的 时 候，你 又 认 为 甲 真 不
zé yǐ de shí hou nǐ yòu rèn wéi jiǎ zhēn bù

错。
cuò

那 么， 有 没 有 什 么 好 方 法 可 以
nà me yǒu méi yǒu shén me hǎo fāng fǎ kě yǐ

让 你 不 痛 苦 呢? 好 像 没 有。 不 过，
ràng nǐ bù tòng kǔ ne hǎo xiàng méi yǒu bù guò

在 中 国 的 古 书 上， 有 个 女 孩 子
zài zhōng guó de gǔ shū shàng yǒu gè nǚ hái zi

在 两 个 男 孩 子 中 间 选 丈 夫 的
zài liǎng gè nán hái zi zhōng jiān xuǎn zhàng fū de

故 事， 我 们 来 看 看 她 是 怎 么 做
gù shì wǒ men lái kàn kan tā shì zěn me zuò

的。
de

这 个 女 孩 子 叫 小 丽， 小 丽 很 漂
zhè gè nǚ hái zi jiào Xiǎo Lì Xiǎo Lì hěn piào

亮 也 很 聪 明。 她 左 右 两 家 邻 居
liang yě hěn cōng míng tā zuǒ yòu liǎng jiā lín jū

的 男 孩 子 一 起 向 她 求 婚。 左 边
de nán hái zi yī qǐ xiàng tā qiú hūn zuǒ biān

那 家 的 男 孩 子 长 得 很 英 俊， 但
nà jiā de nán hái zi zhǎng de hěn yīng jùn dàn

是 很 穷; 右 边 那 家 的 男 孩 子 长
shì hěn qióng yòu biān nà jiā de nán hái zi zhǎng

得 很 丑, 但 是 很 富。
de hěn chǒu dàn shì hěn fù

小 丽 的 父 母 很 难 决 定 把 女 儿
Xiǎo Lì de fù mǔ hěn nán jué dìng bǎ nǚ ér

嫁 给 谁, 就 问 小 丽 想 跟 谁 结 婚。
jià gěi shéi jiù wèn Xiǎo Lì xiǎng gēn shéi jié hūn

小 丽 低 头 半 天 不 说 话。 小 丽 的
Xiǎo Lì dī tóu bàn tiān bù shuō huà Xiǎo Lì de

爸 爸 妈 妈 就 对 她 说, 你 要 是 不
bà ba mā ma jiù duì tā shuō nǐ yào shì bù

好 意 思 说 出 来 的 话, 你 就 举 一
hǎo yì si shuō chū lái de huà nǐ jiù jǔ yī

下 手。 如 果 你 想 跟 左 边 邻 居 家
xià shǒu rú guǒ nǐ xiǎng gēn zuǒ biān lín jū jiā

的 孩 子 结 婚, 你 就 举 左 手; 如 果
de hái zi jié hūn nǐ jiù jǔ zuǒ shǒu rú guǒ

你 愿 意 跟 右 边 邻 居 家 的 孩 子
nǐ yuàn yì gēn yòu biān lín jū jiā de hái zi

结 婚, 你 就 举 右 手。
jié hūn nǐ jiù jǔ yòu shǒu

小 丽 想 了 一 会 儿, 慢 慢 地 举 起
Xiǎo Lì xiǎng le yī huì er màn màn de jǔ qǐ

了 双 手。 她 的 父 母 觉 得 很 奇 怪
le shuāng shǒu tā de fù mǔ jué de hěn qí guài

就 问 小 丽: 你 为 什 么 举 起 两 只
jiù wèn Xiǎo Lì nǐ wèi shén me jǔ qǐ liǎng zhī

手 呢? 小 丽 回 答 说:"我 想 在 右 边
shǒu ne Xiǎo Lì huí dá shuō wǒ xiǎng zài yòu biān

的 邻 居 家 吃 饭, 在 左 边 的 邻 居
de lín jū jiā chī fàn zài zuǒ biān de lín jū

家 睡 觉。"
jiā shuì jiào

# 三

不　听　话　的　太　阳
bù　tīng　huà　de　tài　yáng

---

很　久　以　前，天　上　有　十　个　太　阳。太
hěn　jiǔ　yǐ　qián　tiān　shàng　yǒu　shí　gè　tài　yáng　tài

阳　每　天　从　东　边　走　到　西　边，给　人
yáng　měi　tiān　cóng　dōng　biān　zǒu　dào　xī　biān　gěi　rén

们　带　来　光　明，带　来　温　暖。
men　dài　lái　guāng　míng　dài　lái　wēn　nuǎn

那　时　候，上　帝　规　定　每　天　只　能　有
nà　shí　hou　Shàng　dì　guī　dìng　měi　tiān　zhǐ　néng　yǒu

一　个　太　阳　出　来，因　为　如　果　十　个
yī　gè　tài　yáng　chū　lái　yīn　wèi　rú　guǒ　shí　gè

太　阳　一　起　出　来　的　话，太　多　的　热
tài　yáng　yī　qǐ　chū　lái　de　huà　tài　duō　de　rè

就　会　给　人　们　带　来　灾　害。
jiù　huì　gěi　rén　men　dài　lái　zāi　hài

一　天，太　阳　们　突　然　觉　得　每　天　只
yī　tiān　tài　yáng　men　tú　rán　jué　de　měi　tiān　zhǐ

是　一　个　太　阳　出　去　走　太　寂　寞　了，
shì　yī　gè　tài　yáng　chū　qù　zǒu　tài　jì　mò　le

没　有　一　点　儿　乐　趣，于　是　她　们　就
méi　yǒu　yī　diǎn　er　lè　qù　yú　shì　tā　men　jiù

一　起　出　去　了。
yī　qǐ　chū　qù　le

当 十 个 太 阳 一 起 出 来 的 时 候，
dāng shí gè tài yáng yī qǐ chū lái de shí hou

天 气 就 变 得 非 常 热。不 一 会 儿，
tiān qì jiù biàn de fēi cháng rè bù yī huì er

花 儿 热 死 了，树 木 热 死 了，最 后
huā er rè sǐ le shù mù rè sǐ le zuì hòu

连 河 里 的 水 都 被 太 阳 晒 干 了。
lián hé lǐ de shuǐ dōu bèi tài yáng shài gān le

人 们 热 得 受 不 了 了，就 去 告 诉
rén men rè de shòu bù liǎo le jiù qù gào sù

上 帝。上 帝 让 太 阳 们 赶 快 回 去。
Shàng dì Shàng dì ràng tài yáng men gǎn kuài huí qù

可 是 太 阳 们 不 听 上 帝 的 话，她
kě shì tài yáng men bù tīng Shàng dì de huà tā

们 在 外 面 跑 来 跑 去，谁 也 不 愿
men zài wài miàn pǎo lái pǎo qù shéi yě bù yuàn

意 回 去。
yì huí qù

上 帝 看 到 人 们 都 快 要 热 死 了，
Shàng dì kàn dào rén men dōu kuài yào rè sǐ le

他 很 生 气，于 是 命 令 后 羿 把 十
tā hěn shēng qì yú shì mìng lìng Hòu yì bǎ shí

个 太 阳 全 都 杀 死。
gè tài yáng quán dōu shā sǐ

后羿是一个很有名的猎人，他
Hòu yì shì yī gè hěn yǒu míng de liè rén， tā
射箭射得很好。后羿看到十个
shè jiàn shè de hěn hǎo。 Hòu yì kàn dào shí gè
太阳出来害人，也非常生气，就
tài yáng chū lái hài rén， yě fēi cháng shēng qì， jiù
带着弓箭爬到山上，把太阳一
dài zhe gōng jiàn pá dào shān shang， bǎ tài yáng yī
个一个地射了下来。
gè yī gè de shè le xià lái

当后羿射下第九个太阳的时
dāng Hòu yì shè xià dì jiǔ gè tài yáng de shí
候，他突然想到，要是没有太阳，
hou， tā tū rán xiǎng dào， yào shì méi yǒu tài yáng，
世界上就没有光明和温暖，那
shì jiè shang jiù méi yǒu guāng míng hé wēn nuǎn， nà
样人们也就没有办法生活了，
yàng rén men yě jiù méi yǒu bàn fǎ shēng huó le，
于是他就留下了最后一个太
yú shì tā jiù liú xià le zuì hòu yī gè tài
阳。
yáng

后羿为人们做了一件好事情，
Hòu yì wèi rén men zuò le yī jiàn hǎo shì qing，
大家都很感谢他，希望他能永
dà jiā dōu hěn gǎn xiè tā， xī wàng tā néng yǒng

远 帮 助 人 们， 于 是 上 帝 就 给 了
yuǎn bāng zhù rén men yú shì Shàng dì jiù gěi le

后 羿 一 颗 "不 死 药"，这 颗 "不 死 药"
Hòu yì yī kē bù sǐ yào zhè kē bù sǐ yào

可 以 让 人 长 生 不 老， 永 远 不 死。
kě yǐ ràng rén cháng shēng bù lǎo yǒng yuǎn bù sǐ

# 四

月　宫　里　的　嫦　娥
yuè　gōng　li　de　Cháng　é

---

后　羿　的　妻　子　叫　嫦　娥，嫦　娥　长　得
Hòu　yì　de　qī　zi　jiào　Cháng　é，Cháng　é　zhǎng　de

又　漂　亮　又　聪　明。嫦　娥　知　道　上　帝
yòu　piào　liàng　yòu　cōng　míng。Cháng　é　zhī　dào　Shàng　dì

给　了　后　羿　一　颗　"不　死　药"，她　心　想:
gěi　le　Hòu　yì　yī　kē　"bù　sǐ　yào"，tā　xīn　xiǎng:

人　永　远　活　着　多　好　啊! 谁　愿　意　死
rén　yǒng　yuǎn　huó　zhe　duō　hǎo　a! shéi　yuàn　yì　sǐ

呢? !
ne

一　天，嫦　娥　趁　后　羿　不　在　家　的　时
yī　tiān，Cháng　é　chèn　Hòu　yì　bù　zài　jiā　de　shí

候，偷　偷　地　把　那　颗　"不　死　药"　吃　了
hou，tōu　tōu　de　bǎ　nà　kē　"bù　sǐ　yào"　chī　le

下　去。嫦　娥　把　药　吃　下　去　以　后，突
xià　qù。Cháng　é　bǎ　yào　chī　xià　qù　yǐ　hòu，tū

然　发　觉　自　己　的　身　体　变　轻　了，而
rán　fā　jué　zì　jǐ　de　shēn　tǐ　biàn　qīng　le，ér

且　越　来　越　轻。渐　渐　地　嫦　娥　升　到
qiě　yuè　lái　yuè　qīng。jiàn　jiàn　de　Cháng　é　shēng　dào

了　天　空　中，飞　到　了　月　亮　上。这　时
le　tiān　kōng　zhōng，fēi　dào　le　yuè　liang　shang。zhè　shí

候 嫦 娥 才 明 白，"不 死 药"原 来 是
hou Cháng é cái míng bai bù sǐ yào yuán lái shì

让 人 永 远 活 在 天 上 的。
ràng rén yǒng yuǎn huó zài tiān shang de

嫦 娥 飞 到 月 亮 上 以 后，就 住 在
Cháng é fēi dào yuè liang shang yǐ hòu jiù zhù zài

月 宫 里。月 宫 很 大，也 很 漂 亮。月
yuè gōng lǐ yuè gōng hěn dà yě hěn piāo liang yuè

宫 的 院 子 里 有 一 棵 高 大 的 桂
gōng de yuàn zi li yǒu yī kē gāo dà de guì

花 树，树 底 下 还 有 一 只 可 爱 的
huā shù shù dǐ xià hái yǒu yī zhī kě ài de

小 白 兔。嫦 娥 每 天 什 么 事 情 都
xiǎo bái tù Cháng é měi tiān shén me shì qing dōu

不 做，只 是 唱 歌，跳 舞。
bù zuò zhǐ shì chàng gē tiào wǔ

过 了 一 段 时 间 以 后，嫦 娥 就 觉
guò le yī duàn shí jiān yǐ hòu Cháng é jiù jué

得 没 有 意 思 了。月 宫 虽 然 很 大，
de méi yǒu yì si le yuè gōng suī rán hěn dà

可 是 没 有 人 跟 她 一 起 住；这 里
kě shì méi yǒu rén gēn tā yī qǐ zhù zhè li

虽 然 有 香 甜 的 桂 花 酒，可 是 没
suī rán yǒu xiāng tián de guì huā jiǔ kě shì méi

有 人 跟 她 一 起 喝。月 亮 上 没 有
yǒu rén gēn tā yī qǐ hē yuè liang shang méi yǒu

人 和 她 说 话；没 有 人 听 她 唱 歌；
rén hé tā shuō huà méi yǒu rén tīng tā chàng gē

也 没 有 人 跟 她 跳 舞，嫦 娥 一 个
yě méi yǒu rén gēn tā tiào wǔ Cháng é yī gè

人 感 到 很 寂 寞。
rén gǎn dào hěn jì mò

这 时 候，她 想 起 了 她 的 丈 夫 后
zhè shí hou tā xiǎng qǐ le tā de zhàng fu Hòu

羿，想 起 了 以 前 的 邻 居，想 起 了
yì xiǎng qǐ le yǐ qián de lín jū xiǎng qǐ le

许 多 好 朋 友。嫦 娥 心 里 很 难 过，
xǔ duō hǎo péng yǒu Cháng é xīn lǐ hěn nán guò

她 后 悔 自 己 偷 吃 了 "不 死 药"。
tā hòu huǐ zì jǐ tōu chī le bù sǐ yào

一 年 又 一 年，很 多 年 过 去 了，嫦
yī nián yòu yī nián hěn duō nián guò qù le Cháng

娥 一 个 人 呆 在 冷 冰 冰 的 月 宫
é yī gè rén dāi zài lěng bīng bīng de yuè gōng

里。她 常 常 在 想：每 当 月 亮 圆 的
lǐ tā cháng cháng zài xiǎng měi dāng yuè liang yuán de

时 候，人 们 就 望 着 月 亮，望 着 月
shí hou rén men jiù wàng zhe yuè liang wàng zhe yuè

宫 里 的 我。很 多 人 羡 慕 我，都 以
gōng li de wǒ hěn duō rén xiàn mù wǒ dōu yǐ

为 我 很 快 乐，我 很 幸 福。
wéi wǒ hěn kuài lè wǒ hěn xìng fú

其实，我是一个很可怜的人。我
qí shí, wǒ shì yī gè hěn kě lián de rén。 wǒ

不想呆在月亮上了，我要回到
bù xiǎng dāi zài yuè liang shang le, wǒ yào huí dào

人间去。现在如果有一颗药能
rén jiān qù。 xiàn zài rú guǒ yǒu yī kē yào néng

让我回去，我一定……。
ràng wǒ huí qù, wǒ yī dìng ……。

# 五

喜 欢 吃 中 国 菜
xǐ huān chī Zhōng guó cài

---

外 国 人 喜 欢 吃 中 国 菜， 他 们 说
wài guó rén xǐ huān chī Zhōng guó cài， tā men shuō

中 国 菜 又 好 吃 又 便 宜。 在 外 国
Zhōng guó cài yòu hǎo chī yòu pián yi。 zài wài guó

人 看 来， 不 管 是 上 海 饭 馆 还 是
rén kàn lái， bù guǎn shì shàng hǎi fàn guǎn hái shì

四 川 餐 厅， 中 国 菜 的 味 道 差 不
sì chuān cān tīng， Zhōng guó cài de wèi dào chā bù

多 都 一 样。 其 实， 中 国 不 同 地 方
duō dōu yī yàng。 qí shí， Zhōng guó bù tóng dì fāng

的 菜 有 不 同 的 味 道。 比 如 上 海
de cài yǒu bù tóng de wèi dào。 bǐ rú Shàng hǎi

菜 比 较 甜， 陕 西 菜 比 较 咸， 四 川
cài bǐ jiào tián， Shǎn xī cài bǐ jiào xián， Sì chuān

菜 比 较 辣， 山 西 菜 比 较 酸。
cài bǐ jiào là， Shān xī cài bǐ jiào suān。


中 国 菜 很 早 就 随 着 中 国 移 民
Zhōng guó cài hěn zǎo jiù suí zhe Zhōng guó yí mín

来 到 了 海 外。 那 时 海 外 的 中 国
lái dào le hǎi wài。 nà shí hǎi wài de Zhōng guó

人 比 较 少， 到 中 国 饭 馆 吃 饭 的
rén bǐ jiào shǎo， dào Zhōng guó fàn guǎn chī fàn de

大都是外国人。中国饭馆为了
dà dū shì wài guó rén。Zhōng guó fàn guǎn wèi le

适应外国人的口味就改变一
shì yìng wài guó rén de kǒu wèi jiù gǎi biàn yī

些菜的味道，结果许多中国饭
xiē cài de wèi dào，jié guǒ xǔ duō Zhōng guó fàn

馆的菜不再是地道的中国菜
guǎn de cài bù zài shì dì dào de Zhōng guó cài

了，而且不管是上海饭馆，还是
le，ér qiě bù guǎn shì Shàng hǎi fàn guǎn，hái shì

四川餐厅，菜的味道都差不多
Sì chuān cān tīng，cài de wèi dào dōu chà bù duō

一样。
yī yàng。

现在海外的中国人多起来了，
xiàn zài hǎi wài de Zhōng guó rén duō qǐ lái le，

有些中国饭馆就做出了味道
yǒu xiē Zhōng guó fàn guǎn jiù zuò chū le wèi dào

和样式完全不同的两种菜，准
hé yàng shì wán quán bù tóng de liǎng zhǒng cài，zhǔn

备了两种不同的菜单。给中国
bèi le liǎng zhǒng bù tóng de cài dān。gěi Zhōng guó

人吃的是地道的中国菜，给外
rén chī de shì dì dào de Zhōng guó cài，gěi wài

国人吃的是洋化了的中国菜。
guó rén chī de shì yáng huà le de Zhōng guó cài。

外国人知道中国人吃饭用筷
wài guó rén zhī dào Zhōng guó rén chī fàn yòng kuài

子，于 是 他 们 吃 中 国 饭 时 也 用
zi yú shì tā men chī Zhōng guó fàn shí yě yòng

筷 子。 其 实， 中 国 人 很 早 以 前 也
kuài zi qí shí Zhōng guó rén hěn zǎo yǐ qián yě

是 用 刀 叉 吃 饭 的， 只 是 后 来 人
shì yòng dāo chā chī fàn de zhǐ shì hòu lái rén

们 觉 得 刀 叉 是 武 器， 在 饭 桌 上
men jué de dāo chā shì wǔ qì zài fàn zhuō shang

不 文 明， 才 改 用 筷 子 的。
bù wén míng cái gǎi yòng kuài zi de

中 国 人 吃 饭 会 发 出 一 些 呼 噜
Zhōng guó rén chī fàn huì fā chū yī xiē hū lū

呼 噜 的 响 声， 特 别 是 吃 面 条 和
hū lū de xiǎng shēng tè bié shì chī miàn tiáo hé

喝 稀 饭 的 时 候， 人 们 觉 得 吃 饭
hē xī fàn de shí hou rén men jué de chī fàn

有 呼 噜 呼 噜 的 响 声 才 表 明 饭
yǒu hū lū hū lū de xiǎng shēng cái biǎo míng fàn

菜 做 得 好 吃。
cài zuò de hǎo chī

中 国 人 吃 饭 可 以 发 出 响 声， 但
Zhōng guó rén chī fàn kě yǐ fā chū xiǎng shēng dàn

是 吃 饭 的 时 候 不 许 说 话， 孔 子
shì chī fàn de shí hou bù xǔ shuō huà kǒng zǐ

三 千 年 以 前 就 说 过："食 不 语， 寝
sān qiān nián yǐ qián jiù shuō guò shí bù yǔ qǐn

不 言", 意 思 是 说 吃 饭 和 睡 觉 的
bù yán yì si shì shuō chī fàn hé shuì jiào de

时 候 都 不 许 说 话。可 是 不 知 道
shí hou dōu bù xǔ shuō huà kě shì bù zhī dào

为 什 么, 在 中 国 餐 馆 你 常 常 可
wèi shén me zài Zhōng guó cān guǎn nǐ cháng cháng kě

以 看 到 许 多 人 坐 在 饭 桌 前, 一
yǐ kàn dào xǔ duō rén zuò zài fàn zhuō qián yī

边 儿 吃 饭, 一 边 儿 大 声 说 话。
biān er chī fàn yī biān er dà shēng shuō huà

# 六

中　国　画　儿　里　有　意　思
Zhōng guó huà er li yǒu yì si

---

只　要　有　中　国　人　的　地　方　就　有　中
zhǐ yào yǒu Zhōng guó rén de dì fang jiù yǒu Zhōng

国　画　儿。中　国　人　特　别　喜　欢　中　国
guó huà er Zhōng guó rén tè bié xǐ huān Zhōng guó

画　儿，这　是　因　为　中　国　画　儿　不　仅
huà er zhè shì yīn wèi Zhōng guó huà er bù jǐn

好　看，而　且　画　儿　里　面　的　花　啊、鸟
hǎo kàn ér qiě huà er li miàn de huā a niǎo

啊、树　啊、人　啊　什　么　的，都　有　一　些
a shù a rén a shén me de dōu yǒu yī xiē

特　殊　的　含　义。
tè shū de hán yì

例　如:人　们　喜　欢　画　着　许　多　大　牡
lì rú rén men xǐ huān huà zhe xǔ duō dà mǔ

丹　花　的　画　儿，这　幅　画　儿　叫　做　"荣
dān huā de huà er zhè fú huà er jiào zuò róng

华　富　贵"。中　国　人　认　为　牡　丹　花　代
huá fù guì Zhōng guó rén rèn wéi mǔ dān huā dài

表　着　大　福　大　贵，人　们　喜　欢　牡　丹
biǎo zhe dà fú dà guì rén men xǐ huān mǔ dān

花，就是希望自己今后也能大
huā jiù shì xī wàng zì jǐ jīn hòu yě néng dà

福大贵。
fú dà guì

老人们都喜欢画着松树和仙
lǎo rén men dōu xǐ huān huà zhe sōng shù hé xiān

鹤的画儿，这幅画儿叫做"松鹤
hè de huà er zhè fú huà er jiào zuò sōng hè

延年"。松树和仙鹤可以活很长
yán nián sōng shù hé xiān hè kě yǐ huó hěn cháng

时间，"松鹤延年"意思是祝愿老
shí jiān sōng hè yán nián yì si shì zhù yuàn lǎo

人像松树和仙鹤那样健康、长
rén xiàng sōng shù hé xiān hè nà yàng jiàn kāng cháng

寿。
shòu

新婚夫妇的家里都挂有鸳鸯
xīn hūn fū fù de jiā li dōu guà yǒu yuān yāng

游水的画儿，这幅画儿的意思
yóu shuǐ de huà er zhè fú huà er de yì si

是说夫妻两人要像鸳鸯那样
shì shuō fū qī liǎng rén yào xiàng yuān yāng nà yàng

白头到老。据说一对鸳鸯到老
bái tóu dào lǎo jù shuō yī duì yuān yāng dào lǎo

都不会分离的。
dōu bù huì fēn lí de

如果 一 幅 画儿 上 画 着 两 只 喜
rú guǒ yī fú huà er shang huà zhe liǎng zhī xǐ

鹊 飞 到 家 门 口， 这 幅 画儿 就 叫
què fēi dào jiā mén kǒu zhè fú huà er jiù jiào

做 "双 喜 临 门"。 从 古 到 今， 所 有 的
zuò shuāng xǐ lín mén cóng gǔ dào jīn suǒ yǒu de

中 国 人 都 喜 欢 喜 鹊， 就 是 因 为
Zhōng guó rén dōu xǐ huān xǐ què jiù shì yīn wèi

喜 鹊 的 "喜" 字 和 喜 事 的 "喜" 字 是
xǐ què de xǐ zì hé xǐ shì de xǐ zì shì

同 一 个 字， "双 喜 临 门" 这 幅 画儿
tóng yī gè zì shuāng xǐ lín mén zhè fú huà er

的 意 思 是 说 两 件 喜 事 一 起 来
de yì si shì shuō liǎng jiàn xǐ shì yī qǐ lái

到 家 里 了。
dào jiā li le

有 时 候 你 也 会 觉 得 很 奇 怪， 一
yǒu shí hou nǐ yě huì jué de hěn qí guài yī

幅 漂 亮 的 画儿 上 面 怎 么 有 几
fú piào liàng de huà er shàng mian zěn me yǒu jǐ

只 很 难 看 的 蝙 蝠 呢? 原 来 蝙 蝠
zhī hěn nán kàn de biān fú ne yuán lái biān fú

的 "蝠" 和 福 气 的 "福" 读 音 一 样， 画儿
de fú hé fú qì de fú dú yīn yī yàng huà

上 有 了 蝙 蝠， 意 思 是 说 你 的
er shang yǒu le biān fú yì si shì shuō nǐ de

福 气 就 要 到 了。
fú qì jiù yào dào le

中 国 画 儿 表 达 了 人 们 美 好 的
Zhōng guó huà er biǎo dá le rén men měi hǎo de

希 望 和 祝 愿。 现 在 不 但 中 国 人
xī wàng hé zhù yuàn xiàn zài bù dàn Zhōng guó rén

喜 欢 中 国 画 儿， 就 连 外 国 人 也
xǐ huān Zhōng guó huà er jiù lián wài guó rén yě

都 喜 欢 又 好 看 又 有 深 刻 含 义
dōu xǐ huān yòu hǎo kàn yòu yǒu shēn kè hán yì

的 中 国 画 儿 了。
de Zhōng guó huà er le

# 七

太阳 的 远 近
tài yáng de yuǎn jìn

孔 子 是 中 国 历 史 上 有 名 的 思
Kǒng zǐ shì Zhōng guó lì shǐ shang yǒu míng de sī
想 家、教 育 家。孔 子 很 有 学 问，很
xiǎng jiā jiào yù jiā Kǒng zǐ hěn yǒu xué wèn hěn
多 事 情 他 都 知 道，所 以 大 家 都
duō shì qing tā dōu zhī dào suǒ yǐ dà jiā dōu
非 常 尊 敬 他，把 他 叫 做 圣 人。
fēi cháng zūn jìng tā bǎ tā jiào zuò shèng rén

一 天，孔 子 坐 车 去 旅 行，在 路 上
yī tiān Kǒng zǐ zuò chē qù lǚ xíng zài lù shang
他 看 到 路 边 儿 有 两 个 小 孩 子
tā kàn dào lù biān er yǒu liǎng gè xiǎo hái zi
大 声 地 争 论 着 什 么，于 是 就 下
dà shēng de zhēng lùn zhe shén me yú shì jiù xià
车 走 过 去 问 小 孩 子："小 朋 友，你
chē zǒu guò qù wèn xiǎo hái zi xiǎo péng yǒu nǐ
们 在 争 论 什 么 呢？"
men zài zhēng lùn shén me ne

两 个 小 孩 子 看 到 孔 子 来 了 都
liǎng gè xiǎo hái zi kàn dào Kǒng zǐ lái le dōu

非 常 高 兴, 就 一 起 问 孔 子 说: "先
fēi cháng gāo xìng jiù yī qǐ wèn Kǒng zǐ shuō xiān

生, 您 说 太 阳 早 上 离 我 们 近, 还
sheng nín shuō tài yáng zǎo shang lí wǒ men jìn hái

是 中 午 离 我 们 近? "
shì zhōng wǔ lí wǒ men jìn

一 个 小 孩 子 还 没 有 等 孔 子 回
yī gè xiǎo hái zi hái méi yǒu děng Kǒng zǐ huí

答, 就 抢 着 说: "当 然 是 早 上 离 我
dá jiù qiǎng zhe shuō dāng rán shì zǎo shang lí wǒ

们 近 了。 您 看, 早 上 的 太 阳 就 和
men jìn le nín kàn zǎo shang de tài yáng jiù hé

您 车 上 的 伞 盖 一 样 大, 可 是 中
nín chē shang de sǎn gài yī yàng dà kě shì zhōng

午 的 太 阳 却 只 有 小 盘 子 那 么
wǔ de tài yáng què zhǐ yǒu xiǎo pán zi nà me

大。 这 不 就 是 远 的 东 西 显 得 小,
dà zhè bù jiù shì yuǎn de dōng xi xiǎn de xiǎo

近 的 东 西 显 得 大 的 道 理 吗? "
jìn de dōng xi xiǎn de dà de dào lǐ ma

孔 子 刚 要 点 头 说 对, 另 一 个 小
Kǒng zǐ gāng yào diǎn tóu shuō duì lìng yī gè xiǎo

孩 子 赶 紧 说: "不 对, 不 对! 先 生 您
hái zi gǎn jǐn shuō bù duì bù duì xiān sheng nín

想 想， 早 晨 太 阳 刚 出 来 的 时 候，
xiǎng xiǎng zǎo chén tài yáng gāng chū lái de shí hou

天 气 很 凉， 可 是 到 了 中 午 的 时
tiān qì hěn liáng kě shì dào le zhōng wǔ de shí

候， 天 气 就 很 热 了。 这 不 就 是 离
hou tiān qì jiù hěn rè le zhè bù jiù shì lí

热 的 东 西 近 就 觉 得 热， 离 热 的
rè de dōng xi jìn jiù jué de rè lí rè de

东 西 远 就 觉 得 凉 的 道 理 吗？"
dōng xi yuǎn jiù jué de liáng de dào lǐ ma

孔 子 觉 得 这 个 小 孩 子 说 的 也
Kǒng zǐ jué de zhè gè xiǎo hái zi shuō de yě

对。 他 想 了 一 会 儿， 认 为 两 个 小
duì tā xiǎng le yī huì er rèn wéi liǎng gè xiǎo

孩 子 说 的 都 有 道 理。 这 个 时 候
hái zi shuō de dōu yǒu dào lǐ zhè gè shí hou

孔 子 也 糊 涂 了， 他 也 弄 不 清 楚
Kǒng zǐ yě hú tu le tā yě nòng bù qīng chǔ

太 阳 到 底 是 早 上 近， 还 是 中 午
tài yáng dào dǐ shì zǎo shang jìn hái shì zhōng wǔ

近。
jìn

两 个 小 孩 子 看 到 孔 子 连 这 么
liǎng gè xiǎo hái zi kàn dào Kǒng zǐ lián zhè me

简 单 的 事 情 都 不 知 道， 就 一 起
jiǎn dān de shì qing dōu bù zhī dào jiù yī qǐ

笑 了 起 来，说："哎 呀！谁 说 您 什 么
xiào le qǐ lái shuō āi yā shéi shuō nín shén me

都 知 道 啊？您 原 来 跟 我 们 一 样
dōu zhī dào a nín yuán lái gēn wǒ men yī yàng

啊！"
a

# 八

自 以 为 聪 明 的 人
zì yǐ wéi cōng míng de rén

---

世 上 有 许 多 聪 明 人，也 有 许 多
shì shang yǒu xǔ duō cōng míng rén yě yǒu xǔ duō

自 以 为 聪 明 的 人。聪 明 人 做 事
zì yǐ wéi cōng míng de rén cōng míng rén zuò shì

情 的 时 候，会 想 出 一 些 办 法 来，
qing de shí hou huì xiǎng chū yī xiē bàn fǎ lái

把 事 情 做 得 又 快 又 好；自 以 为
bǎ shì qing zuò de yòu kuài yòu hǎo zì yǐ wéi

聪 明 的 人 做 事 情 的 时 候，也 会
cōng míng de rén zuò shì qing de shí hou yě huì

想 一 些 办 法，但 是 他 们 想 出 来
xiǎng yī xiē bàn fǎ dàn shì tā men xiǎng chū lái

的 办 法，常 常 把 事 情 办 坏。下 面
de bàn fǎ cháng cháng bǎ shì qing bàn huài xià miàn

讲 的 就 是 一 个 自 以 为 聪 明 的
jiǎng de jiù shì yī gè zì yǐ wéi cōng míng de

人 做 笨 事 情 的 故 事。
rén zuò bèn shì qing de gù shi


很 久 以 前 有 个 人 叫 李 明，有 一
hěn jiǔ yǐ qián yǒu gè rén jiào Lǐ Míng yǒu yī

年 他 帮 朋 友 照 看 庄 稼。李 明 天
nián tā bāng péng yǒu zhào kàn zhuāng jia Lǐ Míng tiān

天 去 田 里 看 小 秧 苗 长 高 了 没
tiān qù tián li kàn xiǎo yāng miáo zhǎng gāo le méi

有， 每 次 去 的 时 候 他 都 觉 得 小
yǒu měi cì qù de shí hou tā dōu jué de xiǎo

秧 苗 长 得 太 慢 了， 好 像 总 是 那
yāng miáo zhǎng de tài màn le hǎo xiàng zǒng shì nà

么 一 点 点 儿 高， 李 明 有 些 着 急
me yī diǎn diǎn er gāo Lǐ Míng yǒu xiē zháo jí

了。
le

李 明 要 想 办 法 让 小 秧 苗 长 得
Lǐ Míng yào xiǎng bàn fǎ ràng xiǎo yāng miáo zhǎng de

快 一 点 儿， 长 得 高 一 些。 这 天 晚
kuài yī diǎn er zhǎng de gāo yī xiē zhè tiān wǎn

上 他 躺 在 床 上 翻 来 覆 去 地 想
shang tā tǎng zài chuáng shang fān lái fù qù de xiǎng

啊、 想 啊 ……， 天 快 亮 的 时 候， 他 终
a xiǎng a tiān kuài liàng de shí hou tā zhōng

于 想 出 来 了 一 个 好 办 法： 把 小
yú xiǎng chū lái le yī gè hǎo bàn fǎ bǎ xiǎo

秧 苗 拔 高 一 点 儿。
yāng miáo bá gāo yī diǎn er

想 到 这 个 办 法 以 后， 李 明 非 常
xiǎng dào zhè gè bàn fǎ yǐ hòu Lǐ Míng fēi cháng

兴 奋， 他 觉 得 自 己 很 聪 明， 很 了
xīng fèn tā jué de zì jǐ hěn cōng míng hěn liǎo

不 起。 他 自 言 自 语 地 说： "小 秧 苗
bù qǐ tā zì yán zì yǔ de shuō xiǎo yāng miáo

长 得 慢， 我 们 可 以 帮 助 它 长 快
zhǎng de màn wǒ men kě yǐ bāng zhù tā zhǎng kuài

一 点 儿 啊! 大 家 怎 么 这 么 笨 呢?
yī diǎn er a dà jiā zěn me zhè me bèn ne

怎 么 连 这 么 简 单 的 办 法 都 想
zěn me lián zhè me jiǎn dān de bàn fǎ dōu xiǎng

不 到 呢? "
bù dào ne

李 明 兴 奋 得 睡 不 着 觉 了。 天 刚
Lǐ Míng xīng fèn de shuì bù zháo jiào le tiān gāng

刚 亮， 他 就 跑 到 田 么 去， 一 个 人
gāng liàng tā jiù pǎo dào tián li qù yī gè rén

弯 着 腰 把 小 秧 苗 一 棵 一 棵 地
wān zhe yāo bǎ xiǎo yāng miáo yī kē yī kē de

往 高 拔。 他 拔 啊、 拔 啊……, 从 早 上
wǎng gāo bá tā bá a bá a cóng zǎo shang

一 直 拔 到 天 黑。 当 田 里 剩 下 最
yī zhí bá dào tiān hēi dāng tián li shèng xià zuì

后 几 棵 秧 苗 的 时 候, 李 明 累 得
hòu jǐ kē yāng miáo de shí hou Lǐ Míng lèi de

实 在 拔 不 动 了, 他 直 起 腰 来, 摇
shí zài bá bù dòng le tā zhí qǐ yāo lái yáo

摇 晃 晃 地 回 家 去 了。
yáo huàng huàng de huí jiā qù le

第 二 天 一 大 早， 李 明 就 来 到 田
dì èr tiān yī dà zǎo Lǐ Míng jiù lái dào tián

里 看 他 的 秧 苗。 他 发 现 昨 天 辛
li kàn tā de yāng miáo tā fā xiàn zuó tiān xīn

辛 苦 苦 拔 高 的 秧 苗 全 都 死 了，
xīn kǔ kǔ bá gāo de yāng miáo quán dōu sǐ le

只 有 那 几 棵 没 有 拔 的 小 秧 苗
zhǐ yǒu nà jǐ kē méi yǒu bá de xiǎo yāng miáo

直 直 地 站 立 着， 这 时 候 他 突 然
zhí zhí de zhàn lì zhe zhè shí hou tā tū rán

觉 得 这 几 棵 秧 苗 一 夜 之 间 好
jué de zhè jǐ kē yāng miáo yī yè zhī jiān hǎo

像 长 高 了 许 多。
xiàng zhǎng gāo le xǔ duō

# 九

要 有 礼 貌 地 称 呼 人
yào yǒu lǐ mào de chēng hu rén

---

中 国 人 在 称 呼 上 特 别 讲 究 礼
Zhōng guó rén zài chēng hu shàng tè bié jiǎng jiu lǐ

貌。他 们 在 问 别 人 姓 什 么 的 时
mào tā men zài wèn bié rén xìng shén me de shí

候，会 很 有 礼 貌 地 说："您 贵 姓？"如
hou huì hěn yǒu lǐ mào de shuō nín guì xìng rú

果 问 的 是 一 位 年 纪 很 大 的 人，
guǒ wèn de shì yī wèi nián jì hěn dà de rén

他 们 还 会 更 有 礼 貌 地 说："老 人
tā men hái huì gèng yǒu lǐ mào de shuō lǎo rén

家，您 老 贵 姓？"
jiā nín lǎo guì xìng

中 国 人 喜 欢 用 家 庭 成 员 的 称
Zhōng guó rén xǐ huān yòng jiā tíng chéng yuán de chēng

谓 来 称 呼 那 些 年 纪 大 的 人，比
wèi lái chēng hu nà xiē nián jì dà de rén bǐ

如 说，见 到 跟 父 母 年 纪 差 不 多
rú shuō jiàn dào gēn fù mǔ nián jì chā bu duō

大 的 人，就 要 叫 人 家 叔 叔、阿 姨，
dà de rén jiù yào jiào rén jia shū shu ā yí

伯 伯、伯 母；要 是 见 到 年 纪 更 大
bó bo bó mǔ yào shì jiàn dào nián jì gèng dà

的 人，就 叫 人 家 爷 爷、奶 奶。用 家
de rén jiù jiào rén jiā yé ye nǎi nai yòng jiā

庭 成 员 的 称 谓 来 称 呼 年 纪 大
tíng chéng yuán de chēng wèi lái chēng hu nián jì dà

的 人，也 是 一 种 礼 貌 的 做 法。
de rén yě shì yī zhǒng lǐ mào de zuò fǎ

父 母 教 育 孩 子 要 尊 敬 大 人。他
fù mǔ jiào yù hái zi yào zūn jìng dà rén tā

们 告 诉 孩 子 叫 人 的 时 候 要 注
men gào sù hái zi jiào rén de shí hou yào zhù

意 年 龄，千 万 别 叫 错 了。如 果 遇
yì nián líng qiān wàn bié jiào cuò le rú guǒ yù

到 一 个 人，你 弄 不 清 楚 应 该 叫
dào yī gè rén nǐ nòng bù qīng chǔ yīng gāi jiào

他 哥 哥，还 是 叫 他 叔 叔，那 么 就
tā gē ge hái shì jiào tā shū shu nà me jiù

叫 他 叔 叔；弄 不 清 楚 应 该 叫 他
jiào tā shū shu nòng bù qīng chǔ yīng gāi jiào tā

叔 叔，还 是 叫 他 爷 爷，那 么 就 叫
shū shu hái shì jiào tā yé ye nà me jiù jiào

他 爷 爷。总 之，要 往 高 叫，往 高 叫
tā yé ye zǒng zhī yào wǎng gāo jiào wǎng gāo jiào

也 表 示 一 种 礼 貌。
yě biǎo shì yī zhǒng lǐ mào

父母们还特别告诉孩子，一定
fù mǔ men hái tè bié gào sù hái zi, yī dìng
不能叫年纪大的人的名字。中
bù néng jiào nián jì dà de rén de míng zì Zhōng
国人认为，叫年纪大的人的名
guó rén rèn wéi, jiào nián jì dà de rén de míng
字是最不礼貌的做法。当然，对
zì shì zuì bù lǐ mào de zuò fǎ dāng rán, duì
于坏人，即使是年纪大的人，也
yú huài rén, jí shǐ shì nián jì dà de rén, yě
不能叫他们叔叔、阿姨、爷爷、奶
bù néng jiào tā men shū shu ā yí yé ye nǎi
奶什么的。
nai shén me de

西方国家的称呼习惯跟中国
Xī fāng guó jiā de chēng hu xí guàn gēn Zhōng guó
不完全一样，西方国家的小孩
bù wán quán yī yàng, Xī fāng guó jiā de xiǎo hái
子有时候可以直接叫大人的
zi yǒu shí hòu kě yǐ zhí jiē jiào dà rén de
名字。在西方国家的中小学里，
míng zì zài xī fāng guó jiā de zhōng xiǎo xué li
学生和大人一样都把老师叫
xué sheng hé dà rén yī yàng dōu bǎ lǎo shī jiào
做"先生、女士"或者"小姐"什么的。
zuò "xiān sheng nǚ shì" huò zhě "xiǎo jiě" shén me de

在 中 国 的 学 校 里，特 别 是 中 小
zài Zhōng guó de xué xiào li， tè bié shì zhōng xiǎo

学 里，学 生 一 定 得 很 尊 敬 地 把
xué li， xué sheng yī dìng de hěn zūn jìng de bǎ

老 师 叫 做 "老 师"。如 果 一 个 学 生
lǎo shī jiào zuò lǎo shī。 rú guǒ yī gè xué sheng

随 随 便 便 地 把 老 师 叫 "先 生、女
suí suí biàn biàn de bǎ lǎo shī jiào xiān sheng nǚ

士、小 姐" 的 话，他 恐 怕 就 得 不 到
shì xiǎo jiě de huà， tā kǒng pà jiù dé bù dào

好 成 绩 了。
hǎo chéng jī le

# 十

独 生 子 女 长 大 了
dú shēng zǐ nǚ zhǎng dà le

---

中 国 现 在 有 十 三 亿 多 人, 是 世
Zhōng guó xiàn zài yǒu shí sān yì duō rén, shì shì

界 上 人 口 最 多 的 国 家。 中 国 政
jiè shàng rén kǒu zuì duō de guó jiā zhōng guó zhèng

府 为 了 控 制 人 口 增 长, 1979 年 制
fǔ wèi le kòng zhì rén kǒu zēng zhǎng nián zhì

定 了 一 项 计 划 生 育 政 策, 这 个
dìng le yī xiàng jì huà shēng yù zhèng cè zhè gè

政 策 规 定 每 个 家 庭 只 能 生 一
zhèng cè guī dìng měi gè jiā tíng zhǐ néng shēng yī

个 孩 子。 从 那 以 后, 在 中 国 出 生
gè hái zi cóng nà yǐ hòu zài Zhōng guó chū shēng

的 孩 子 大 都 是 没 有 兄 弟 姐 妹
de hái zi dà dōu shì méi yǒu xiōng dì jiě mèi

的 "独 生 子 女"。
de dú shēng zǐ nǚ

中 国 人 的 传 统 思 想 是 传 宗 接
Zhōng guó rén de chuán tǒng sī xiǎng shì chuán zōng jiē

代, 意 思 是 要 自 己 的 子 孙 一 代
dài, yì si shì yào zì jǐ de zǐ sūn yī dài

接 一 代 地 延 续 下 去。 这 就 是 千
jiē yī dài de yán xù xià qù zhè jiù shì qiān

**180** | 拼音课文

百 年 来 中 国 人 想 多 生 孩 子， 特
bǎi nián lái Zhōng guó rén xiǎng duō shēng hái zi tè

别 想 多 生 男 孩 子 的 原 因， 这 也
bié xiǎng duō shēng nán hái zi de yuán yīn zhè yě

是 中 国 人 口 越 来 越 多 的 原 因。
shì Zhōng guó rén kǒu yuè lái yuè duō de yuán yīn

现 在 一 个 家 庭 只 能 生 一 个 孩
xiàn zài yī gè jiā tíng zhǐ néng shēng yī gè hái

子， 这 个 孩 子 就 成 了 家 里 的 宝
zi zhè gè hái zi jiù chéng le jiā li de bǎo

贝， 爸 爸、 妈 妈、 爷 爷、 奶 奶、 外 公、 外
bèi bà ba mā ma yé ye nǎi nai wài gōng wài

婆， 所 有 人 都 宠 爱 这 个 孩 子。 因
pó suǒ yǒu rén dōu chǒng ài zhè gè hái zi yīn

为 家 里 人 都 围 着 独 生 子 女 转，
wèi jiā li rén dōu wéi zhe dú shēng zǐ nǚ zhuàn

人 们 就 把 独 生 子 女 叫 做 "小 太
rén men jiù bǎ dú shēng zǐ nǚ jiào zuò xiǎo tài

阳"； 因 为 家 里 人 都 特 别 宠 爱 独
yáng yīn wèi jiā li rén dōu tè bié chǒng ài dú

生 子 女， 大 家 也 就 把 独 生 子 女
shēng zǐ nǚ dà jiā yě jiù bǎ dú shēng zǐ nǚ

叫 做 "小 皇 帝"。
jiào zuò xiǎo huáng dì

有 人 担 心 这 些 独 生 子 女 长 大
yǒu rén dān xīn zhè xiē dú shēng zǐ nǚ zhǎng dà

以 后 会 变 得 比 较 自 私， 他 们 可
yǐ hòu huì biàn de bǐ jiào zì sī tā men kě

能 会 没 有 朋 友，会 很 孤 独。也 有
néng huì méi yǒu péng yǒu huì hěn gū dú yě yǒu

人 说 不 用 担 心，因 为 当 每 一 个
rén shuō bù yòng dān xīn yīn wèi dāng měi yī gè

孩 子 都 是 小 太 阳 的 时 候，他 们
hái zi dōu shì xiǎo tài yáng de shí hou tā men

谁 都 不 是 小 太 阳 了；当 每 一 个
shéi dōu bù shì xiǎo tài yáng le dāng měi yī gè

孩 子 都 是 小 皇 帝 的 时 候，他 们
hái zi dōu shì xiǎo huáng dì de shí hou tā men

谁 也 都 不 是 小 皇 帝 了。
shéi yě dōu bù shì xiǎo huáng dì le

今 天，中 国 有 八 千 多 万 个 独 生
jīn tiān Zhōng guó yǒu bā qiān duō wàn gè dú shēng

子 女，他 们 中 许 多 都 已 经 长 大
zǐ nǚ tā men zhōng xǔ duō dōu yǐ jīng zhǎng dà

成 人 了。这 些 长 大 了 的 独 生 子
chéng rén le zhè xiē zhǎng dà le de dú shēng zǐ

女 并 不 像 人 们 担 心 的 那 样 自
nǚ bìng bù xiàng rén men dān xīn de nà yàng zì

私、孤 独，他 们 有 很 多 朋 友。而 且，
sī gū dú tā men yǒu hěn duō péng yǒu ér qiě

由 于 很 多 独 生 子 女 从 小 受 到
yóu yú hěn duō dú shēng zǐ nǚ cóng xiǎo shòu dào

很 好 的 教 育，所 以 他 们 在 工 作
hěn hǎo de jiào yù suǒ yǐ tā men zài gōng zuò

和 生 活 中 也 显 得 比 较 能 干。
hé shēng huó zhōng yě xiǎn de bǐ jiào néng gàn

当然，他们也有自己的弱点，由
dāng rán tā men yě yǒu zì jǐ de ruò diǎn yóu

于他们从小被过分地宠爱，所
yú tā men cóng xiǎo bèi guò fēn dì chǒng ài suǒ

以在遇到困难时就显得有些
yǐ zài yù dào kùn nán shí jiù xiǎn de yǒu xiē

无能为力，而且和别人相处时
wú néng wéi lì ér qiě hé bié rén xiāng chǔ shí

常常喜欢以自己为中心。
cháng cháng xǐ huān yǐ zì jǐ wéi zhōng xīn

◆ 附录二 练习答案 ◆
附錄二 練習答案 ◆

Answer Key

<table>
<tr><td colspan="2">一. ✦ 小霞的网恋 ✦<br>◆ 小霞的網戀 ◆</td></tr>
</table>

一、

1. 遇到 — 碰见
   遇到 — 碰見
2. 从早到晚 — 整天
   從早到晚 — 整天
3. 来往 — 交朋友
   來往 — 交朋友
4. 聊天儿 — 谈话
   聊天兒 — 談話
5. 马上 — 立刻
   馬上 — 立刻
6. 一定 — 肯定
   一定 — 肯定

二、

1. b
2. a
3. c
4. b

三、

1. b
2. b
3. a
4. c

# 二. ◆ 小丽想跟谁結婚 ◆
## ◆ 小麗想跟誰結婚 ◆

一、

1. 左 — 右
   左 — 右
2. 幸福 — 痛苦
   幸福 — 痛苦
3. 英俊 — 丑
   英俊 — 醜
4. 結婚 — 离婚
   結婚 — 離婚
5. 甲 — 乙
   甲 — 乙
6. 违法 — 合法
   違法 — 合法

二、

1. b
2. c
3. a
4. c

三、

1. c
2. a
3. c
4. b

# 三. ◆ 不听话的太阳 ◆
## ◆ 不聽話的太陽 ◆

一、

1. 长生不老 — 永远不死
   長生不老 — 永遠不死
2. 受不了了 — 不能忍受
   受不了了 — 不能忍受
3. 不一会儿 — 很短时间
   不一會兒 — 很短時間
4. 带来灾害 — 带来不幸
   帶來災害 — 帶來不幸
5. 没有乐趣 — 太寂寞了
   沒有樂趣 — 太寂寞了
6. 跑来跑去 — 东跑西跑
   跑來跑去 — 東跑西跑

二、

1. b
2. c
3. a
4. c

三、

1. c
2. a
3. b
4. c

## 四. ✦ 月宮里的嫦娥 ✦
✦ 月宮裡的嫦娥 ✦

**一、**

1. 漂亮 — 难看
   漂亮 — 難看
2. 突然 — 渐渐地
   突然 — 漸漸地
3. 冰冷 — 温暖
   冰冷 — 溫暖
4. 人间 — 天上
   人間 — 天上
5. 快乐 — 难过
   快樂 — 難過
6. 香甜 — 难吃
   香甜 — 難吃

**二、**

1. c
2. b
3. c
4. a

**三、**

1. b
2. c
3. b
4. a

五.

# 五. ◆ 喜欢吃中国菜 ◆
## ◆ 喜歡吃中國菜 ◆

一、

    1. 餐馆 — 饭馆
       餐館 — 飯館
    2. 筷子 — 刀叉
       筷子 — 刀叉
    3. 地道 — 洋化
       地道 — 洋化
    4. 面条 — 稀饭
       麵條 — 稀飯
    5. 甜酸 — 咸辣
       甜酸 — 咸辣
    6. 上海 — 四川
       上海 — 四川

二、

    1. c
    2. b
    3. a
    4. b

三、

    1. a
    2. c
    3. b
    4. b

六． ◆ 中国画儿里有意思 ◆
◆ 中國畫兒裡有意思 ◆

一、

1. 特殊 — 意思
　　特殊 — 意思
2. 健康 — 长寿
　　健康 — 長壽
3. 荣华 — 富贵
　　榮華 — 富貴
4. 双喜 — 临门
　　雙喜 — 臨門
5. 白头 — 到老
　　白頭 — 到老
6. 松鹤 — 延年
　　松鶴 — 延年

二、

1. c
2. a
3. b
4. a

三、

1. b
2. a
3. b
4. c

# 七. ◆ 太阳的远近 ◆
## ◆ 太陽的遠近 ◆

一、

1. 学问 — 知识
   學問 — 知識
2. 认为 — 觉得
   認為 — 覺得
3. 争论 — 辩论
   爭論 — 辯論
4. 清楚 — 明白
   清楚 — 明白
5. 天气 — 气候
   天氣 — 氣候
6. 早上 — 早晨
   早上 — 早晨

二、

1. c
2. b
3. c
4. a

三、

1. b
2. b
3. c
4. a

## 八. ◆ 自以为聪明的人 ◆
## ◆ 自以為聰明的人 ◆

一、

1. 聪明 — 笨
   聰明 — 笨
2. 高 — 低
   高 — 低
3. 躺 — 站
   躺 — 站
4. 简单 — 复杂
   簡單 — 複雜
5. 天黑 — 天亮
   天黑 — 天亮
6. 一点儿 — 许多
   一點兒 — 許多

二、

1. c
2. b
3. a
4. b

三、

1. c
2. a
3. b
4. c

# 九. ✦ 有礼貌的称呼人 ✦
## ✦ 有禮貌的稱呼人 ✦

一、

    1. c

    2. b

    3. a

    4. c

二、

    1. 把跟父母年纪差不多大的人叫 — 叔叔，阿姨。
       伯伯，伯母。
       把跟父母年紀差不多大的人叫 — 叔叔，阿姨，
       伯伯，伯母。

    2. 把比父母年纪大的人叫 — 爷爷，奶奶，外婆，
       外公。
       把比父母年紀大的人叫 — 爺爺，奶奶，外婆，
       外公。

    3. 把比自己年纪大的人叫 — 大哥，大姐。
       把比自己年紀大的人叫 — 大哥，大姐。

    4. 把比自己年纪小的人叫 — 小弟，小妹。
       把比自己年紀小的人叫 — 小弟，小妹。

三、

    1. c

    2. a

    3. b

    4. c

# 十. ◆ 独生子女长大了 ◆
## ◆ 獨生子女長大了 ◆

## 一、

1. 增长 — 减少
   增長 — 減少
2. 传统 — 现代
   傳統 — 現代
3. 子孙 — 祖先
   子孫 — 祖先
4. 能干 — 无能
   能干 — 無能
5. 希望 — 失望
   希望 — 失望
6. 延续 — 停止
   延續 — 停止

## 二、

1. b
2. c
3. a
4. c

## 三、

1. c
2. b
3. b
4. a

# ✦ 生词索引 ✦
## 生词索引

### Vocabulary Index (Alphabetical by Pinyin)

| Pinyin | Simplified Characters | Traditional Characters | Part of Speech | English Definition | Lesson |
|--------|----------------------|------------------------|----------------|--------------------|--------|
| **A** | | | | | |
| āiyā | 哎呀 | 哎呀 | *interj.* | Ah! | 7 |
| āyí | 阿姨 | 阿姨 | *n.* | mother's sister; aunt | 9 |
| **B** | | | | | |
| bá | 拔 | 拔 | *v.* | pull up | 8 |
| bǎi | 百 | 百 | *num.* | hundred | 10 |
| báitóudàolǎo | 白头到老 | 白頭到老 | *id.* | to live together until old age | 6 |
| bǎiwàn | 百万 | 百萬 | *num.* | million | 10 |
| bàn | 办 | 辦 | *v.* | do | 8 |
| bàntiān | 半天 | 半天 | *n.* | a long time; quite a while | 1 |
| bǎobèi | 宝贝 | 寶貝 | *n.* | treasure | 10 |
| bāozi | 包子 | 包子 | *n.* | steamed stuffed bun | 5 |
| běidǒuxīng | 北斗星 | 北斗星 | *n.* | the Big Dipper | 4 |
| bèn | 笨 | 笨 | *adj.* | stupid; foolish | 8 |
| bǐjiào | 比较 | 比較 | *adv.* | comparatively | 5 |
| biānfú | 蝙蝠 | 蝙蝠 | *n.* | bat | 6 |

| Pinyin | Simplified Characters | Traditional Characters | Part of Speech | English Definition | Lesson |
|--------|----------------------|------------------------|----------------|--------------------|--------|
| biànde | 变得 | 變得 | *v.* | change to | 3 |
| biǎodá | 表达 | 表達 | *v.* | express; convey | 6 |
| biǎomíng | 表明 | 表明 | *v.* | make known; indicate | 5 |
| biǎoshì | 表示 | 表示 | *v.* | express; indicate | 9 |
| bùcuò | 不错 | 不錯 | *adj.* | not bad; pretty good | 2 |
| bùhǎoyìsi | 不好意思 | 不好意思 | *adj.* | feel embarrassed | 1 |
| bùjǐn...érqiě | 不仅…而且 | 不僅…而且 | *conj.* | not only...but also | 2 |
| bùsǐyào | 不死药 | 不死藥 | *n.* | immortality elixir | 3 |

**C**

| Pinyin | Simplified Characters | Traditional Characters | Part of Speech | English Definition | Lesson |
|--------|----------------------|------------------------|----------------|--------------------|--------|
| càidān | 菜单 | 菜單 | *n.* | menu | 5 |
| cāixiǎng | 猜想 | 猜想 | *v.* | suppose; guess | 1 |
| Cháng'é | 嫦娥 | 嫦娥 | *prn.* | goddess of the moon | 4 |
| chángshēngbùlǎo | 长生不老 | 長生不老 | *id.* | immortal | 3 |
| chángshòu | 长寿 | 長壽 | *adj.* | long life | 6 |
| cháoshī | 潮湿 | 潮濕 | *adj.* | moist; damp | 3 |
| chèn | 趁 | 趁 | *prep.* | take advantage of | 4 |
| chēnghu | 称呼 | 稱呼 | *n.* | form of address | 9 |
| chēngwèi | 称谓 | 稱謂 | *n.* | appellation; title | 9 |
| chéngjì | 成绩 | 成績 | *n.* | grade; achievement | 9 |
| chéngyuán | 成员 | 成員 | *n.* | member | 9 |
| chónghūn | 重婚 | 重婚 | *n.* | bigamy | 2 |
| chǒngài | 宠爱 | 寵愛 | *adj.* | pamper; dote on | 10 |
| chǒu | 丑 | 醜 | *adj.* | ugly | 2 |
| chūliàn | 初恋 | 初戀 | *n.* | first love | 1 |

| Pinyin | Simplified Characters | Traditional Characters | Part of Speech | English Definition | Lesson |
|---|---|---|---|---|---|
| chuántǒng | 传统 | 傳統 | *n.* | tradition | 10 |
| chuánzǒngjiēdài | 传宗接代 | 傳宗接代 | *id.* | keep the family line alive | 10 |
| cōngyóubǐng | 葱油饼 | 蔥油餅 | *n.* | scallion pancake | 5 |

**D**

| | | | | | |
|---|---|---|---|---|---|
| dǎléi | 打雷 | 打雷 | *n.* | thunder | 3 |
| dàbó | 大伯 | 大伯 | *n.* | a polite form of address to an elderly man | 9 |
| dàfúdàguì | 大福大贵 | 大福大貴 | *adj* | good fortune and high rank | 6 |
| dàgē | 大哥 | 大哥 | *n.* | a polite form of address to a man about one's own age | 9 |
| dàjiě | 大姐 | 大姐 | *n.* | a polite form of address to a woman about one's own age | 9 |
| dàmā | 大妈 | 大媽 | *n.* | a polite form of address to an elderly woman | 9 |
| dàmǐ | 大米 | 大米 | *n.* | (husked) rice | 8 |
| dàniáng | 大娘 | 大娘 | *n.* | a polite form of address to an elderly woman | 9 |
| dàshěn | 大婶 | 大嬸 | *n.* | a polite form of address to an elderly woman | 9 |
| dàshū | 大叔 | 大叔 | *n.* | a polite form of address to an elderly man | 9 |
| dàye | 大爷 | 大爺 | *n.* | a polite form of address to an elderly man | 9 |
| dāi | 呆 | 呆 | *v.* | stay | 4 |
| dài | 代 | 代 | *n.* | generation | 10 |
| dàibiǎo | 代表 | 代表 | *v.* | represent | 6 |
| dàilái | 带来 | 帶來 | *vc.* | bring to | 3 |

| Pinyin | Simplified Characters | Traditional Characters | Part of Speech | English Definition | Lesson |
|--------|----------------------|----------------------|----------------|-------------------|--------|
| dāngrán | 当然 | 當然 | *adv.* | of course | 7 |
| dāng...shíhou | 当···时候 | 當···時候 | *prep.* | when | 2 |
| dāochā | 刀叉 | 刀叉 | *n.* | knife and fork | 5 |
| dàodé | 道德 | 道德 | *n.* | morals; morality | 2 |
| dàoli | 道理 | 道理 | *n.* | principle; truth | 7 |
| dàodǐ | 到底 | 到底 | *adv.* | after all; in the end | 7 |
| dàozi | 稻子 | 稻子 | *n.* | rice; paddy | 8 |
| dītóu | 低头 | 低頭 | *vo.* | lower (or bow) one's head | 2 |
| dìqiú | 地球 | 地球 | *n.* | the earth; the globe | 4 |
| dìdào | 地道 | 地道 | *adj.* | authentic; genuine | 5 |
| diǎntóu | 点头 | 點頭 | *vo.* | nod one's head | 7 |
| dìnghūn | 订婚 | 訂婚 | *v.* | be engaged (to be married) | 2 |
| dòujiāng | 豆浆 | 豆漿 | *n.* | soy-bean milk | 5 |
| dòuzi | 豆子 | 豆子 | *n.* | beans or peas | 8 |
| dúshēngzǐnǚ | 独生子女 | 獨生子女 | *n.* | the only child | 10 |
| dúyīn | 读音 | 讀音 | *n.* | pronunciation | 6 |
| duìyú | 对于 | 對於 | *prep.* | for | 9 |

## F

| Pinyin | Simplified Characters | Traditional Characters | Part of Speech | English Definition | Lesson |
|--------|----------------------|----------------------|----------------|-------------------|--------|
| fāchū xiǎngshēng | 发出响声 | 發出響聲 | *vo.* | emit a sound | 5 |
| fājué | 发觉 | 發覺 | *v.* | find; detect | 4 |
| fāxiàn | 发现 | 發現 | *v.* | find; discover | 8 |
| fā xìn | 发信 | 發信 | *vo.* | post a letter | 1 |
| fānláifùqù | 翻来复去 | 翻來復去 | *id.* | toss and turn | 8 |
| fāngbiànmiàn | 方便面 | 方便麵 | *n.* | instant noodles | 5 |

| Pinyin | Simplified Characters | Traditional Characters | Part of Speech | English Definition | Lesson |
|---|---|---|---|---|---|
| fàngxīn | 放心 | 放心 | *v.* | set one's mind at rest | 1 |
| fēnlí | 分离 | 分離 | *v.* | separate; sever | 6 |
| fēngjǐnghuà | 风景画 | 風景畫 | *n.* | landscape painting | 6 |
| fūqī | 夫妻 | 夫妻 | *n.* | husband and wife | 6 |
| fú | 幅 | 幅 | *m.* | classifier; measure word | 6 |
| fúqi | 福气 | 福氣 | *n.* | happy lot; good fortune | 6 |
| fù | 富 | 富 | *adj.* | rich; wealthy | 2 |

**G**

| Pinyin | Simplified Characters | Traditional Characters | Part of Speech | English Definition | Lesson |
|---|---|---|---|---|---|
| gǎiyòng | 改用 | 改用 | *v.* | to shift to use | 5 |
| gǎnjǐn | 赶紧 | 趕緊 | *adv.* | immediately | 7 |
| gǎnkuài | 赶快 | 趕快 | *adj.* | at once; quickly | 1 |
| gānzào | 干燥 | 乾燥 | *adj.* | dry; arid | 3 |
| gè | 个 | 個 | *m.* | unit; measure word | 10 |
| gōngjiàn | 弓箭 | 弓箭 | *n.* | bow and arrow | 3 |
| gūdú | 孤独 | 孤獨 | *adj.* | lonely; solitary | 10 |
| gǔshū | 古书 | 古書 | *n.* | ancient books | 2 |
| guāfēng | 刮风 | 颳風 | *adj.* | windy | 3 |
| guà | 挂 | 掛 | *v.* | hang | 6 |
| guāngmíng | 光明 | 光明 | *n.* | light; bright | 3 |
| guīdìng | 规定 | 規定 | *v.* | rule; ordain | 3 |
| guìhuāshù | 桂花树 | 桂花樹 | *n.* | sweet-scented osmanthus bush | 4 |
| guōtiē | 锅贴 | 鍋貼 | *n.* | fried dumpling | 5 |
| guòfèn | 过分 | 過分 | *adj.* | excessive; over | 10 |

| Pinyin | Simplified Characters | Traditional Characters | Part of Speech | English Definition | Lesson |
|--------|----------------------|------------------------|----------------|--------------------|--------|
| **H** | | | | | |
| hǎiwài | 海外 | 海外 | *n.* | overseas; abroad | 5 |
| hài | 害 | 害 | *v.* | injure; harm | 3 |
| hàipà | 害怕 | 害怕 | *v.* | be scared | 1 |
| hánlěng | 寒冷 | 寒冷 | *adj.* | cold; frigid | 3 |
| hányì | 含义 | 含義 | *n.* | meaning; implication | 6 |
| héqì | 和气 | 和氣 | *adj.* | kind; polite | 1 |
| hóngshǔ | 红薯 | 紅薯 | *n.* | yam | 8 |
| hǒuhuǐ | 后悔 | 後悔 | *v.* | regret; repent | 4 |
| Hòuyì | 后羿 | 后羿 | *prn.* | person's name | 3 |
| hūlū | 呼噜 | 呼嚕 | *n.* | the slurping sound | 5 |
| hútu | 胡涂 | 糊塗 | *adj.* | confuse | 7 |
| huāniǎohuà | 花鸟画 | 花鳥畫 | *n.* | painting of flowers and birds | 6 |
| huàxuéjiā | 化学家 | 化學家 | *n.* | chemist | 7 |
| huàirén | 坏人 | 壞人 | *n.* | bad person | 1 |
| huángdì | 皇帝 | 皇帝 | *n.* | emperor | 10 |
| huánghūnliàn | 黄昏恋 | 黃昏戀 | *n.* | love between an elderly couple | 1 |
| hūnlǐ | 婚礼 | 婚禮 | *n.* | wedding ceremony | 2 |
| hūnwàiliàn | 婚外恋 | 婚外戀 | *n.* | an extramarital love affair | 1 |
| hūnyīn | 婚姻 | 婚姻 | *n.* | marriage; matrimony | 2 |
| húntun | 馄饨 | 餛飩 | *n.* | dumpling soup | 5 |
| **J** | | | | | |
| jíshǐ...yě | 即使…也 | 即使…也 | *conj.* | even if | 9 |
| jìhuàshēngyù | 计划生育 | 計劃生育 | *n.* | birth control | 10 |
| jìmò | 寂寞 | 寂寞 | *adj.* | lonely | 3 |

| Pinyin | Simplified Characters | Traditional Characters | Part of Speech | English Definition | Lesson |
|--------|----------------------|------------------------|----------------|--------------------|--------|
| jiātíng | 家庭 | 家庭 | *n.* | family | 9 |
| jiǎ | 甲 | 甲 | *n.* | the first of the ten Heavenly Stems | 2 |
| jià | 嫁 | 嫁 | *v.* | (of a woman) marry | 2 |
| jiǎndān | 简单 | 簡單 | *adj.* | simple | 7 |
| jiànjiànde | 渐渐地 | 漸漸地 | *adv.* | gradually; little by little | 4 |
| jiànkāng | 健康 | 健康 | *adj.* | health | 6 |
| jiànmiàn | 见面 | 見面 | *v.* | meet; see | 1 |
| jiǎngjiu | 讲究 | 講究 | *v.* | pay attention to; stress | 9 |
| jiǎozi | 饺子 | 餃子 | *n.* | dumpling | 5 |
| jiào rén | 叫人 | 叫人 | *vo.* | address somebody respectfully | 9 |
| jiàoyù | 教育 | 教育 | *v.* | educate | 9 |
| jiàoyùjiā | 教育家 | 教育家 | *n.* | educator | 7 |
| jiéhūn | 结婚 | 結婚 | *v.* | marry; get married | 1 |
| jīnhūn | 金婚 | 金婚 | *n.* | gold wedding (50th anniversary) | 2 |
| jǐnzhāng | 紧张 | 緊張 | *adj.* | nervous | 1 |
| jīngjìxuéjiā | 经济学家 | 經濟學家 | *n.* | economist | 7 |
| jiǔ | 酒 | 酒 | *n.* | wine | 4 |
| jǔ shǒu | 举手 | 舉手 | *vo.* | raise one's hand or hands | 2 |
| jùshuō | 据说 | 據說 | *prep.* | it is said; they say | 6 |
| juéde | 觉得 | 覺得 | *v.* | feel; think | 1 |
| juédìng | 决定 | 決定 | *v./n.* | decide; decision | 2 |

**K**

| | | | | | |
|--------|----------------------|------------------------|----------------|--------------------|--------|
| kēxuéjiā | 科学家 | 科學家 | *n.* | scientist | 7 |
| kěài | 可爱 | 可愛 | *adj.* | lovable; lovely | 4 |

| Pinyin | Simplified Characters | Traditional Characters | Part of Speech | English Definition | Lesson |
|--------|----------------------|------------------------|----------------|--------------------|--------|
| kělián | 可怜 | 可憐 | *adj.* | pitiful | 4 |
| kěndìng | 肯定 | 肯定 | *adv.* | certainly; definitely | 1 |
| kǒngpà | 恐怕 | 恐怕 | *adv.* | (I'm) afraid that; perhaps | 9 |
| kòngzhì | 控制 | 控制 | *v.* | control | 10 |
| kǒuwèi | 口味 | 口味 | *n.* | a person's taste (for food) | 5 |
| kuàilè | 快乐 | 快樂 | *adj.* | happy; joyful | 4 |
| kùnnan | 困难 | 困難 | *n.* | difficulty | 10 |

**L**

| | | | | | |
|--------|----------------------|------------------------|----------------|--------------------|--------|
| là | 辣 | 辣 | *adj.* | hot; (of smell or taste) burn | 5 |
| láiwang | 来往 | 來往 | *v.* | contact | 1 |
| làihūn | 赖婚 | 賴婚 | *v.* | repudiate a marriage contract | 2 |
| lǎodàniáng | 老大娘 | 老大娘 | *n.* | a polite form of address to an elderly woman | 9 |
| lǎodàye | 老大爷 | 老大爺 | *n.* | a polite form of address to an elderly man | 9 |
| lǎonǎinai | 老奶奶 | 老奶奶 | *n.* | a polite form of address to an elderly woman | 9 |
| lǎorénjia | 老人家 | 老人家 | *n.* | a polite form of address to an elderly person | 9 |
| lǎoyéye | 老爷爷 | 老爺爺 | *n.* | a polite form of address to an elderly man | 9 |
| lèqù | 乐趣 | 樂趣 | *n.* | delight; pleasure; joy | 3 |
| lěngbīngbīng | 冷冰冰 | 冷冰冰 | *adj.* | ice-cold; freezing | 4 |
| lí | 离 | 離 | *v.* | away; from | 7 |
| líhūn | 离婚 | 離婚 | *v.* | divorce | 2 |

| Pinyin | Simplified Characters | Traditional Characters | Part of Speech | English Definition | Lesson |
|---|---|---|---|---|---|
| lǐmào | 礼貌 | 禮貌 | *n.* | courtesy | 9 |
| lìshǐ | 历史 | 歷史 | *n.* | history | 7 |
| lián | 连 | 連 | *conj.* | even | 3 |
| liànài | 恋爱 | 戀愛 | *v.* | be in love; have a love affair | 1 |
| liáng | 凉 | 涼 | *adj.* | cold | 7 |
| liángshi | 粮食 | 糧食 | *n.* | grain; cereals | 8 |
| liángshuang | 凉爽 | 涼爽 | *adj.* | pleasantly cool | 3 |
| liáotiānr | 聊天儿 | 聊天兒 | *v.* | chat | 1 |
| liǎobuqǐ | 了不起 | 了不起 | *adj.* | extraordinary; unbelievable | 8 |
| lièrén | 猎人 | 獵人 | *n.* | hunter | 3 |
| línjū | 邻居 | 鄰居 | *n.* | neighbor | 2 |
| liúxià | 留下 | 留下 | *v.* | keep; remain | 3 |
| liúxīng | 流星 | 流星 | *n.* | meteor; shooting star | 4 |
| lǚxíng | 旅行 | 旅行 | *v.* | travel | 7 |

**M**

| | | | | | |
|---|---|---|---|---|---|
| màizi | 麦子 | 麥子 | *n.* | wheat | 8 |
| mántou | 馒头 | 饅頭 | *n.* | steamed bun | 5 |
| mànhuà | 漫画 | 漫畫 | *n.* | caricature; cartoon | 6 |
| mǐfàn | 米饭 | 米飯 | *n.* | rice | 5 |
| miànbāo | 面包 | 麵包 | *n.* | bread | 5 |
| miànfěn | 面粉 | 麵粉 | *n.* | wheat flour; flour | 8 |
| miàntiáo | 面条 | 麵條 | *n.* | noodles | 5 |
| mìnglìng | 命令 | 命令 | *v.* | order; command | 3 |
| mǔdanhuā | 牡丹花 | 牡丹花 | *n.* | peony flower | 6 |

| Pinyin | Simplified Characters | Traditional Characters | Part of Speech | English Definition | Lesson |
|--------|----------------------|------------------------|----------------|--------------------|--------|
| **N** | | | | | |
| nándào | 难道 | 難道 | *adv.* | used to reiterate a rhetorical question | 1 |
| nánguò | 难过 | 難過 | *adj.* | sad; feel badly | 4 |
| nénggàn | 能干 | 能幹 | *adj.* | talented; capable | 10 |
| niánjì (líng) | 年纪 (龄) | 年紀 (齡) | *n.* | age | 9 |
| nínlǎo | 您老 | 您老 | *n.* | a polite form of address to an elderly person | 9 |
| nòng | 弄 | 弄 | *v.* | make; do | 7 |
| nòngbūqīngchǔ | 弄不清楚 | 弄不清楚 | *vc.* | can't understand | 9 |
| nuǎnhuo | 暖和 | 暖和 | *v.* | warm up | 3 |
| nǔshì | 女士 | 女士 | *n.* | lady; madam | 9 |
| **P** | | | | | |
| pà | 怕 | 怕 | *v.* | be afraid of | 1 |
| pánzi | 盘子 | 盤子 | *n.* | plate | 7 |
| piányi | 便宜 | 便宜 | *adj.* | cheap; inexpensive | 5 |
| píngshí | 平时 | 平時 | *n.* | ordinary times | 1 |
| **Q** | | | | | |
| qīzi | 妻子 | 妻子 | *n.* | wife | 4 |
| qíshí | 其实 | 其實 | *adv.* | actually; in fact | 4 |
| qízhōng | 其中 | 其中 | *prep.* | among (which, them, etc.) | 2 |
| qíguài | 奇怪 | 奇怪 | *adj.* | strange; surprising | 2 |
| qiān | 千 | 千 | *num.* | thousand | 10 |
| qiānwàn | 千万 | 千萬 | *adv.* | must; make sure to | 9 |
| qiānwàn | 千万 | 千萬 | *num.* | ten million | 10 |

| Pinyin | Simplified Characters | Traditional Characters | Part of Speech | English Definition | Lesson |
|--------|----------------------|------------------------|----------------|--------------------|--------|
| qiānbǐhuà | 铅笔画 | 鉛筆畫 | *n.* | pencil drawing | 6 |
| qiǎngzhe | 抢着 | 搶著 | *v.* | try to have the floor before… | 7 |
| qǐn | 寝 | 寢 | *v.* | sleep | 5 |
| qīng | 轻 | 輕 | *adj.* | light | 4 |
| qīngchǔ | 清楚 | 清楚 | *adj.* | clearly understood; distinct | 7 |
| qíngtiān | 晴天 | 晴天 | *n.* | sunny day | 3 |
| qióng | 穷 | 窮 | *adj.* | poor; poverty-stricken | 2 |
| qiúhūn | 求婚 | 求婚 | *v.* | make an offer of marriage | 2 |
| què | 却 | 卻 | *conj.* | but | 7 |

**R**

| Pinyin | Simplified Characters | Traditional Characters | Part of Speech | English Definition | Lesson |
|--------|----------------------|------------------------|----------------|--------------------|--------|
| rèliàn | 热恋 | 熱戀 | *v.* | be passionately in love | 1 |
| rénjia | 人家 | 人家 | *n.* | other person | 9 |
| rénjiān | 人间 | 人間 | *n.* | human world | 4 |
| rénkǒu | 人口 | 人口 | *n.* | population | 10 |
| rénwù | 人物 | 人物 | *n.* | figure | 6 |
| rénwùhuà | 人物画 | 人物畫 | *n.* | figure painting | 6 |
| rènwéi | 认为 | 認為 | *v.* | think; consider | 6 |
| rìshí | 日食 | 日食 | *n.* | solar eclipse | 4 |
| rónghuáfùguì | 荣华富贵 | 荣華富貴 | *id.* | high rank and great wealth | 6 |
| ruòdiǎn | 弱点 | 弱點 | *adj.* | weakness; weak point | 10 |

**S**

| Pinyin | Simplified Characters | Traditional Characters | Part of Speech | English Definition | Lesson |
|--------|----------------------|------------------------|----------------|--------------------|--------|
| sǎngài | 伞盖 | 傘蓋 | *n.* | umbrella cover (over a cart) | 7 |
| sānjiǎoliànài | 三角恋爱 | 三角戀愛 | *n.* | love triangle | 2 |

| Pinyin | Simplified Characters | Traditional Characters | Part of Speech | English Definition | Lesson |
|---|---|---|---|---|---|
| shāsǐ | 杀死 | 殺死 | *vc.* | kill | 3 |
| shàigān | 晒干 | 曬乾 | *vc.* | dry in the sun | 3 |
| shānshuǐhuà | 山水画 | 山水畫 | *n.* | landscape painting | 6 |
| shǎndiàn | 闪电 | 閃電 | *n.* | lightning | 3 |
| Shàngdì | 上帝 | 上帝 | *n.* | God | 3 |
| shàngwǎng | 上网 | 上網 | *v.* | log onto the internet | 1 |
| shè | 射 | 射 | *v.* | shoot | 3 |
| shèjiàn | 射箭 | 射箭 | *vo.* | shoot an arrow | 3 |
| shēnkè | 深刻 | 深刻 | *adj.* | deep; profound | 6 |
| shēntǐ | 身体 | 身體 | *n.* | body | 4 |
| shēng | 升 | 昇 | *v.* | rise into | 4 |
| shēngqì | 生气 | 生氣 | *v.* | become angry | 3 |
| shēngsǐliàn | 生死恋 | 生死戀 | *n.* | love in life or death | 1 |
| shèngrén | 圣人 | 聖人 | *n.* | sage; wise person | 7 |
| shèngxià | 剩下 | 剩下 | *v.* | be left (over); remain | 8 |
| shīfu | 师傅 | 師傅 | *n.* | master; a polite form of address to people | 9 |
| shīliàn | 失恋 | 失戀 | *v.* | be disappointed in a love affair | 1 |
| shí | 十 | 十 | *num.* | ten | 10 |
| shíwàn | 十万 | 十萬 | *num.* | hundred thousand | 10 |
| shí | 食 | 食 | *v./n.* | eat; food | 5 |
| shízài | 实在 | 實在 | *adv.* | really; in reality | 8 |
| shìjiè | 世界 | 世界 | *n.* | world | 3 |
| shìshang | 世上 | 世上 | *n.* | world | 8 |
| shìyìng | 适应 | 適應 | *v.* | accommodate | 5 |
| shòubùliǎo | 受不了 | 受不了 | *vc.* | unbearable | 3 |

| Pinyin | Simplified Characters | Traditional Characters | Part of Speech | English Definition | Lesson |
|---|---|---|---|---|---|
| shòudào | 受到 | 受到 | *v.* | receive | 10 |
| shùmù | 树木 | 樹木 | *n.* | trees | 3 |
| shùxuéjiā | 数学家 | 數學家 | *n.* | mathematician | 7 |
| shuāngshǒu | 双手 | 雙手 | *n.* | both hands | 2 |
| shuāngxǐlínmén | 双喜临门 | 雙喜臨門 | *id.* | a double blessing has descended upon one's home | 6 |
| shuǐcǎihuà | 水彩画 | 水彩畫 | *n.* | watercolor | 6 |
| shuǐmòhuà | 水墨画 | 水墨畫 | *n.* | ink and water painting | 6 |
| sīxiǎng | 思想 | 思想 | *n.* | thought | 10 |
| sīxiǎngjiā | 思想家 | 思想家 | *n.* | ideologist; thinker | 7 |
| sōnghèyánnián | 松鹤延年 | 松鶴延年 | *id.* | pine and crane (symbols of longevity | 6 |
| sōngshù | 松树 | 松樹 | *n.* | pine tree | 6 |
| suān | 酸 | 酸 | *n.* | sour | 5 |
| suísuíbiànbiàn | 随随便便 | 隨隨便便 | *adj.* | casual | 9 |
| suízhe | 随着 | 隨著 | *v.* | follow | 5 |

**T**

| | | | | | |
|---|---|---|---|---|---|
| tánliànài | 谈恋爱 | 談戀愛 | *vo.* | fall in love | 2 |
| tāng | 汤 | 湯 | *n.* | soup | 5 |
| tǎng | 躺 | 躺 | *v.* | lie | 8 |
| táohūn | 逃婚 | 逃婚 | *v.* | run away from wedding | 2 |
| tèbié | 特别 | 特别 | *adv.* | especially; particularly | 2 |
| tèshū | 特殊 | 特殊 | *adj.* | special | 6 |
| tíchū | 提出 | 提出 | *v.* | put forward; bring up | 1 |
| tiānkōng | 天空 | 天空 | *n.* | the sky | 4 |

| Pinyin | Simplified Characters | Traditional Characters | Part of Speech | English Definition | Lesson |
|--------|----------------------|------------------------|----------------|--------------------|--------|
| tiānliàng | 天亮 | 天亮 | *n.* | daybreak; dawn; daylight | 8 |
| tián | 甜 | 甜 | *adj.* | sweet | 5 |
| tián | 田 | 田 | *n.* | field | 8 |
| tóngshí | 同时 | 同時 | *adv.* | at the same time | 2 |
| tóngxìngliàn | 同性恋 | 同性戀 | *n.* | homosexual love | 1 |
| tóngyì | 同意 | 同意 | *v.* | agree; consent | 1 |
| tóngzhì | 同志 | 同志 | *n.* | comrade | 9 |
| tòngkǔ | 痛苦 | 痛苦 | *adj.* | pain; suffering | 2 |
| tōutōude | 偷偷地 | 偷偷地 | *adv.* | stealthily | 4 |
| tūrán | 突然 | 突然 | *adv.* | suddenly | 3 |
| tǔdòu | 土豆 | 土豆 | *n.* | potato | 8 |
| tù | 兔 | 兔 | *n.* | rabbit | 4 |
| tuìhūn | 退婚 | 退婚 | *v.* | break off an engagement | 2 |

**W**

| | | | | | |
|--------|----------------------|------------------------|----------------|--------------------|--------|
| wānyāo | 弯腰 | 彎腰 | *vo.* | bend one's waist; stoop | 8 |
| wánquán | 完全 | 完全 | *adj.* | complete; completely | 9 |
| wàn | 万 | 萬 | *num.* | ten thousand | 10 |
| wǎng | 往 | 往 | *prep.* | toward | 8 |
| wǎngliàn | 网恋 | 網戀 | *n.* | netlove | 1 |
| wàng | 望 | 望 | *v.* | gaze into the distance | 4 |
| wéi | 围 | 圍 | *v.* | surround | 10 |
| wéifǎ | 违法 | 違法 | *vo.* | break the law; be illegal | 2 |
| wěiqu | 委屈 | 委屈 | *adj.* | feel wronged | 1 |
| wèi | 为 | 為 | *prep.* | for | 3 |
| wèidào | 味道 | 味道 | *n.* | taste; flavor | 5 |

| Pinyin | Simplified Characters | Traditional Characters | Part of Speech | English Definition | Lesson |
|---|---|---|---|---|---|
| wèihūn | 未婚 | 未婚 | *adj.* | unmarried; single | 2 |
| wèixīng | 卫星 | 衛星 | *n.* | satellite; moon; artificial satellite | 4 |
| wēnnuǎn | 温暖 | 溫暖 | *adj.* | warm | 3 |
| wénmíng | 文明 | 文明 | *n.* | civilization | 5 |
| wúnéngwéilì | 无能为力 | 無能為力 | *id.* | powerless; incapable of action | 10 |
| wǔqì | 武器 | 武器 | *n.* | weapon | 5 |
| wùlǐxuéjiā | 物理学家 | 物理學家 | *n.* | physicist | 7 |

**X**

| | | | | | |
|---|---|---|---|---|---|
| xīwàng | 希望 | 希望 | *v.* | hope; wish | 3 |
| xīfàn | 稀饭 | 稀飯 | *n.* | rice soup | 5 |
| xīfāng | 西方 | 西方 | *n.* | Western | 9 |
| xīyánghuà | 西洋画 | 西洋畫 | *n.* | Western painting | 6 |
| xíguàn | 习惯 | 習慣 | *n.* | be accustomed to; be used to | 9 |
| xǐquè | 喜鹊 | 喜鵲 | *n.* | magpie | 6 |
| xiàxuě | 下雪 | 下雪 | *v.* | snow; snowy | 3 |
| xiàyǔ | 下雨 | 下雨 | *v.* | rain; rainy | 3 |
| xiānsheng | 先生 | 先生 | *n.* | mister (Mr.); gentleman; sir | 9 |
| xiānhè | 仙鹤 | 仙鶴 | *n.* | red-crowned crane | 6 |
| xián | 咸 | 鹹 | *adj.* | salty; salted | 5 |
| xiǎnde | 显得 | 顯得 | *v.* | look like; appear to be | 7 |
| xiànmù | 羡慕 | 羨慕 | *v.* | admire; envy | 4 |
| xiāngchǔ | 相处 | 相處 | *v.* | get along (with one another) | 10 |
| xiāngtián | 香甜 | 香甜 | *adj.* | fragrant and sweet | 4 |
| xiàng | 项 | 項 | *m.* | classifier; measure word | 10 |

| Pinyin | Simplified Characters | Traditional Characters | Part of Speech | English Definition | Lesson |
|---|---|---|---|---|---|
| xiǎojie | 小姐 | 小姐 | *n.* | miss; young lady | 9 |
| xiǎomǐ | 小米 | 小米 | *n.* | millet | 8 |
| xīnxīnkǔkǔ | 辛辛苦苦 | 辛辛苦苦 | *adv.* | laboriously; strenuously | 8 |
| xīngfèn | 兴奋 | 興奮 | *adj.* | be excited | 8 |
| xìngfú | 幸福 | 幸福 | *n./adj.* | happiness; happy | 2 |
| xīngxīng | 星星 | 星星 | *n.* | star | 4 |
| xǔ | 许 | 許 | *v.* | allow; permit | 5 |
| xuānchuánhuà | 宣传画 | 宣傳畫 | *n.* | picture poster | 6 |
| xuǎnzé | 选择 | 選擇 | *v.* | select; choose | 2 |
| xuéwen | 学问 | 學問 | *n.* | knowledge | 7 |

**Y**

| | | | | | |
|---|---|---|---|---|---|
| yán | 言 | 言 | *v.* | talk; speak | 5 |
| yánrè | 炎热 | 炎熱 | *adj.* | blistering hot; sizzling | 3 |
| yánxù | 延续 | 延續 | *v.* | continue; go on | 10 |
| yànmài | 燕麦 | 燕麥 | *n.* | oats | 8 |
| yāngmiáo | 秧苗 | 秧苗 | *n.* | rice seedling | 8 |
| yánghuà | 洋化 | 洋化 | *v.* | Westernized | 5 |
| yàngshì | 样式 | 樣式 | *n.* | style | 5 |
| yáoyáohuànghuàng | 摇摇晃晃 | 搖搖晃晃 | *adj.* | tottering; shaky | 8 |
| yīdiǎndiǎnr | 一点点儿 | 一點點兒 | *adj.* | a little | 8 |
| yī duì | 一对 | 一對 | *m.* | a couple | 6 |
| yímín | 移民 | 移民 | *n.* | emigrant; immigrant | 5 |
| yǐ | 乙 | 乙 | *num.* | the second of the ten Heavenly Stems | 2 |
| yǐ...wéi... | 以···为··· | 以···為··· | *conj.* | consider | 10 |

| Pinyin | Simplified Characters | Traditional Characters | Part of Speech | English Definition | Lesson |
|--------|----------------------|------------------------|----------------|--------------------|--------|
| yǐwéi | 以为 | 以為 | v. | think; believe | 4 |
| yǐhūn | 已婚 | 已婚 | adj. | married | 2 |
| yì | 亿 | 億 | num. | hundred million | 10 |
| yìshùjiā | 艺术家 | 藝術家 | n. | artist | 7 |
| yīntiān | 阴天 | 陰天 | n. | overcast sky | 3 |
| yīnyuèjiā | 音乐家 | 音樂家 | n. | musician | 7 |
| yínhé | 银河 | 銀河 | n. | the Milky Way | 4 |
| yínhūn | 银婚 | 銀婚 | n. | silver wedding (25th anniversary) | 2 |
| yīnggāi | 应该 | 應該 | v. | should; ought to | 9 |
| yīngjùn | 英俊 | 英俊 | adj. | handsome | 2 |
| yǒngyuǎn | 永远 | 永遠 | adj. | forever | 3 |
| yóuhuà | 油画 | 油畫 | n. | oil painting | 6 |
| yóutiáo | 油条 | 油條 | n. | deep-fried twisted dough sticks | 5 |
| yóuyú | 由于 | 由於 | prep. | owing to; as a result of | 10 |
| yǒumíng | 有名 | 有名 | adj. | well-known; famous | 7 |
| yǔ | 语 | 語 | v. | talk; speak | 5 |
| yǔzhòu | 宇宙 | 宇宙 | n. | universe; cosmos | 4 |
| yùdào | 遇到 | 遇到 | v. | run into; encounter | 1 |
| yùmǐ | 玉米 | 玉米 | n. | corn | 8 |
| yuānyang | 鸳鸯 | 鴛鴦 | n. | Mandarin duck | 6 |
| yuánlái | 原来 | 原來 | adv. | originally | 7 |
| yuánxiān | 原先 | 原先 | adj. | original | 4 |
| yuǎnjìn | 远近 | 遠近 | n. | distance | 7 |
| yuànyì | 愿意 | 願意 | v. | be willing; want | 1 |
| yuànzi | 院子 | 院子 | n. | yard | 4 |

| Pinyin | Simplified Characters | Traditional Characters | Part of Speech | English Definition | Lesson |
|--------|----------------------|------------------------|----------------|---------------------|--------|
| yuègōng | 月宫 | 月宫 | *n.* | the palace of the moon | 4 |
| yuèqiú | 月球 | 月球 | *n.* | the moon | 4 |
| yuèshí | 月食 | 月食 | *n.* | lunar eclipse | 4 |
| yuèyá | 月牙 | 月牙 | *n.* | crescent moon | 4 |
| yùnqi | 运气 | 運氣 | *n.* | fortune; luck | 1 |
| yǔnxīng | 陨星 | 隕星 | *n.* | meteorite | 4 |
| | | | | | |
| **Z** | | | | | |
| zāihài | 灾害 | 災害 | *n.* | calamity; disaster | 3 |
| zàihūn | 再婚 | 再婚 | *v.* | remarry; marry again | 2 |
| zǎochén | 早晨 | 早晨 | *n.* | (early) morning | 7 |
| zǎoliàn | 早恋 | 早戀 | *v.* | fall in love at an early age | 1 |
| zēngzhǎng | 增长 | 增長 | *v.* | increase; grow | 10 |
| zhànlì | 站立 | 站立 | *v.* | stand erect; stand upright | 8 |
| zhǎng | 长 | 長 | *v.* | grow | 8 |
| zhàngfu | 丈夫 | 丈夫 | *n.* | husband | 4 |
| zháojí | 着急 | 著急 | *adj.* | anxious; worry | 1 |
| zhàokàn | 照看 | 照看 | *v.* | look after; keep an eye on | 8 |
| zhéxuéjiā | 哲学家 | 哲學家 | *n.* | philosopher | 7 |
| zhème | 这么 | 這麼 | *pn.* | so; such | 7 |
| zhēnghūn | 征婚 | 征婚 | *v.* | marriage seeking | 2 |
| zhēnglùn | 争论 | 爭論 | *v.* | argue | 7 |
| zhěngtiān | 整天 | 整天 | *n.* | the whole day; all day | 1 |
| zhèngcè | 政策 | 政策 | *n.* | policy | 10 |
| zhèngfǔ | 政府 | 政府 | *n.* | government | 10 |
| zhèngzhìjiā | 政治家 | 政治家 | *n.* | statesman; politician | 7 |

| Pinyin | Simplified Characters | Traditional Characters | Part of Speech | English Definition | Lesson |
|--------|----------------------|------------------------|----------------|--------------------|--------|
| zhízhí | 直直 | 直直 | *adj.* | straight; upright | 8 |
| zhījiān | 之间 | 之間 | *n.* | between; among; while | 8 |
| zhíjiē | 直接 | 直接 | *adv.* | directly | 9 |
| zhíqǐyāo | 直起腰 | 直起腰 | *v.* | straighten one's back | 8 |
| zhǐyào…jiù | 只要…就 | 只要…就 | *conj.* | if only; so long as | 6 |
| zhìdìng | 制定 | 制定 | *v.* | lay down; formulate | 10 |
| Zhōngguóhuà | 中国画 | 中國畫 | *n.* | Chinese painting | 6 |
| zhōngyú | 终于 | 終於 | *adv.* | finally | 8 |
| zhùyì | 注意 | 注意 | *v.* | pay attention to | 9 |
| zhùyuàn | 祝愿 | 祝愿 | *v.* | wish | 6 |
| zhuānjiā | 专家 | 專家 | *n.* | expert; specialist | 7 |
| zhuàn | 转 | 轉 | *v.* | turn around, rotate | 10 |
| zhuāngjia | 庄稼 | 莊稼 | *n.* | crops | 8 |
| zìcóng | 自从 | 自從 | *prep.* | since | 1 |
| zìsī | 自私 | 自私 | *adj.* | selfish; self-centered | 10 |
| zìyánzìyǔ | 自言自语 | 自言自語 | *v.* | talk to oneself | 8 |
| zìyǐwéi | 自以为 | 自以為 | *v.* | consider one's self | 8 |
| zǒngshì | 总是 | 總是 | *adv.* | always | 8 |
| zǒngzhī | 总之 | 總之 | *conj.* | in a word; in short | 9 |
| zūnjìng | 尊敬 | 尊敬 | *v.* | respect | 7 |
| zuòfa | 做法 | 做法 | *n.* | way of doing things | 9 |
| zuǒyòu | 左右 | 左右 | *n.* | left and right | 2 |